WATERSIDE
In Lancasnire

Alan Shepley

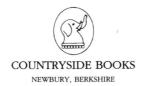

COUNTRYSIDE BOOKS

NEWBURY, BERKSHIRE

COUNTRYSIDE BOOKS
3 Catherine Road
Newbury, Berkshire

ISBN 1 85306 573 0

Designed by Graham Whiteman
Cover illustration by Colin Doggett
Maps and photographs by the author

Produced through MRM Associates Ltd., Reading
Typeset by Techniset Typesetters, Newton-le-Willows
Printed by J. W. Arrowsmith Ltd., Bristol

Contents

AREA MAP SHOWING LOCATIONS OF THE WALKS

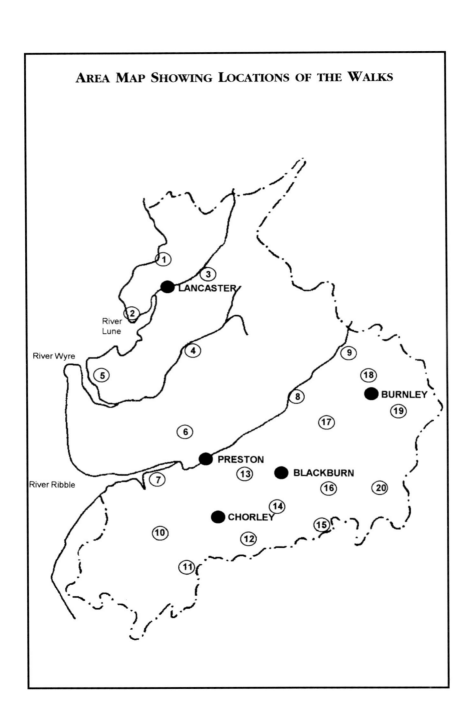

Walk

INTRODUCTION

Lancashire's hill country provides the rain which ultimately gives the opportunity for waterside walks. In the flatlands towards the coast, however, rainfall is relatively low and artificial drainage has removed all the large wetlands and converted them to arable. River, reservoir (and that other artificial construct, the canal), and sea shore all offer enjoyable waterside walking in Lancashire. The major rivers — the east-to-west-flowing Lune, Wyre, Ribble (and its tributaries; the Hodder, Calder, Darwen, and Douglas), and the south-flowing Irwell — provide some fine valley walks. The demands of a rapidly expanding population have resulted in the construction of a large number of reservoirs in Lancashire's hill country right down to recent times. The landscapes around them have often matured into attractive countryside and have become deservedly popular with walkers. Much of the sea coast itself is rather flat and unexciting but the three large estuaries and Morecambe Bay provide a variety which has a salt tang in the air.

In keeping with my other walking guides for Lancashire, the county boundaries have been taken to be those established in 1974. The Boroughs of Blackburn with Darwen and of Blackpool, established in 1998 are, therefore, included in the area.

Each of the walk descriptions is accompanied by a sketch map, and these should enable you to find your way. In each case, however, details of OS maps of 1:25,000 scale, more suitable for use in walking the countryside of Lancashire than the 1:50,000 Landranger series, have been given and these have become more readily accessible in recent years. Many of the walks in this book are now covered by three sheets only — Outdoor Leisure Nos 21 and 41, and the Explorer map No 19. These maps give details of field boundaries and buildings — either of which may have disappeared or been added to since I went that way — and make way-finding easier. On each of the sketch maps the numbers in open circles indicate the sections of the walk description which apply to that part of the route: I hope that this will prove of additional help. Waymarking on the ground has steadily improved over the last decade but there are odd exceptions and occasional patches of poor signing. In accordance with the guidance given by the Outdoor Writers' Guild, all the routes have been walked afresh in the preparation of this book but changes can happen at any time and the publisher would be pleased to hear of any which may be relevant to future editions.

With each walk are suggestions for additional places of interest worth visiting in the immediate locality. The walks themselves have been deliberately kept the sort of distance you might cover in a couple of hours or so — depending, of course, on what you find to catch your interest on the way! (In most instances, there are alternative shorter routes indicated also.) Combining a walk with one, or more, of the other suggestions will readily make a day of it.

Where the occasional hazard is known to exist it has been indicated e.g. old quarry workings, and tides, but there is no substitute for keeping your eyes open and gathering information from local people as you pass — in any case, the latter invariably adds to the enjoyment of a walk. The weather, especially in the hills, can change quickly and footwear with a good grip and rainproof clothing is often essential, even on short walks. An additional hazard arises because, on the whole, domestic pets and farm stock do not mix. Do remember that it is your dog which is the visitor and that the only entitlement is to use the Public Right of Way, not the surrounding land.

Not only do walk route details change, but those for the pubs referred to can change also, perhaps even more frequently. The information given is as accurate as possible at the time of writing but landlords, their policies, and their menus and opening hours are not permanent fixtures and you should check ahead if in any doubt at all. A final Information section is provided to help those who would like to use public transport rather than their car and to enable you to check other tourist details with Information Centres.

Once again, it is a pleasure to thank all those who have helped in the preparation of this book, knowingly and unknowingly. I thank them all most heartily. If, as a result, you join that happy band of wanderers who have derived pleasure from walking in Lancashire's magnificent countryside, and will join with me in wishing to pass it on to future generations as an even better place, it will have been well worth while.

Alan Shepley

KEY TO SKETCH MAPS

· · · · · · · · ——→ · · · · Walk route and suggested direction

Road ———⟨Bridge⟩——— · · · unfenced Road

River   Canal

■ Building

† Church/Chapel

Broadleaved   Coniferous
Woodland   Woodland

Mixed Woodland

Lake or
Reservoir

Quarry or
cliff edge

Dam/Embankment

—+—+—+—+—+— Railway   FB Footbridge

—+——+——+——+— Old railway   P Car Park

———·———·——— County boundary   ▲ Summit

—×—×—×—×—×— Fence

∿∿∿∿∿∿∿∿∿∿∿ Wall

THE LANCASTER CANAL AND MORECAMBE BAY SHORE

The village of Bolton le Sands is, today, bypassed by the main road and has returned to a sleepier past which the coming of the canal and, later, the railway, disturbed for 150 years or so. The pleasant canal-side stroll links the exposed sea shore of Morecambe Bay with some fine views of the Lakeland and Bowland Fells. Beside the wind-bent thorns on the shore it takes only a little imagination to recall the importance of the old routes across the Bay.

The pub in Main Street, Bolton le Sands

By far and away the biggest change to north Lancashire in the last thousand years was the final abandoning of the crossing of Morecambe Bay sands as the main route for getting to Furness and West Cumbria. The building of the railway, in the 1850s, altered our viewpoint for ever and motor transport has firmly cemented our standpoint as that of landsmen. Before these dramatic changes you

9

had no choice but to experience the edges of Morecambe Bay from that strange, and dangerous, moon-controlled world of tide, sand, and sky which, all too often, proved lethal (and still can). Bolton le Sands was one of those shore communities which, as much as anything else, serviced travellers across the Bay.

The Packet Boat Hotel stands a little up Main Street from the canal bridge in Bolton le Sands village and, no doubt, predates the canal's existence. Indeed, its name refers to the former packet boats of the Irish Sea rather than to canal trade. Food is available here from 11 am to 3 pm and between 5.30 pm and 9 pm, and all day on Saturday and Sunday. The main menu is a straightforward offering including that northern staple of meat and potato pie, peas and gravy — excellent on a cool and blowy day. A variety of sandwiches, toasties, and jacket potatoes meet the requirements of a quicker snack. A selection of sweets and specials of the day are served. This is a Thwaites house with their usual bitters and mild, Carlsberg and Carling lagers, Guinness stout, and both Strongbow and Woodpecker cider on draught. There is an especially good choice of malt whiskies. Outside seating enables you to take advantage of good weather; dogs are welcomed.

Telephone: 01524 824069.

- **HOW TO GET THERE:** Turn inland off the A6 at either end of Bolton le Sands and find the pub close to the canal bridge. The approach from the south inevitably takes you through Lancaster city; from the north, use the M6 junction 35 via Carnforth. The nearest stations are Lancaster and Carnforth. Buses are operated by Stagecoach.
- **PARKING:** Limited parking is available at the pub (please ask). Alternatively use the road to the shore where there is extensive parking, and make the pub the half way point of your walk.
- **LENGTH OF THE WALK:** 3 miles. Map: OS Pathfinder 648 Lancaster & Morecambe (GR 484680).

THE WALK

1. Start by either turning right to the canal bridge, crossing this with care for the traffic, and going down the steps on the left to the towpath or, turn left up Main Street and walk up through the old village to the turn just before the church. Go down right and use the steps at the bridge onto the towpath. The latter way gives an

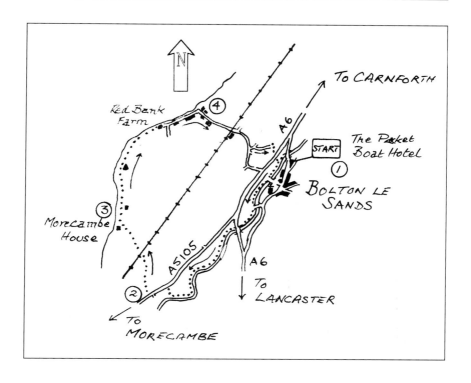

opportunity to glance at St Michael's church, with its 15th century tower, and the older stone buildings in The Nook across the way. Continue along the towpath beside gardens; an old milestone records, enigmatically, '21/6'. The view opens out to the north west across the sands of the mouth of the River Keer, over Morecambe Bay, to Humphrey Head and the southern Cumbrian fells beyond. Ducks and moorhen dabble amongst the weeds by the next bridge, a modern, concrete one with a balustrade, carrying the A6. A wooden swing bridge comes next and gives access across the canal to a large house. Walk round the bend and take the signed path to the right down steps between gardens to reach the main A5105 road to Morecambe.

2. Cross the road with care and use the footway past the bus stop to opposite Greenacre Road on the left. Turn right on the footpath across the field to an iron kissing gate. Bear slightly right to a robust wooden footbridge and make for stepping stones and a stile by the

11

willows. Rise slightly along the line of an old hawthorn hedge to a concrete up-and-over stile and cross the main railway line with great care. Go up the bank to a belt of pine trees and enter the rear of the caravan park. Walk to the right by the grassed circle and between the posts and bear left through the site past the buildings of Morecambe House to a car park at the top of the salt marsh on the shore. Just to the south of here the longest of the old crossings of Morecambe Bay sands begins. (NOTE that the Warning Notice about the tides and quicksands should be heeded and that crossing the Bay is dangerous and should not be attempted without a guide.)

3. The route is now northwards along the track to the stile over the wall near the corner by the gate. Follow the Lancashire Coastal Way sign over the shoulder of Red Bank past windblown thorns and the old OS trig point. Drop down to a second caravan site at Red Bank Farm. Go half left at the stile and steps to more steps at the house end and join the shore road. With the tide out, a potter about the shore is an enjoyable diversion. Walk parallel to the road along the low sea bank and pass toilets and a group of houses with decorative limestone walls to the point at which the road turns inland again.

4. Follow the lane up and round the bends by a third caravan site called Sandside. At St Michael's, the house on the crest, is a fine copper beech tree. Pass by and drop to the railway again. Go over the level crossing with care. Continue up the brow and go left at Monkswell Drive. Bear right into Monkswell Avenue and go forward to meet a footpath beside a stream at the bottom. Turn to the right and follow the stream up beside fruit trees to the main A6. Cross directly over, with care for traffic, and follow the track up the stream beside the restaurant. The track bends left and rises to join the village street beside the canal bridge where you began. Cross back over by Prospect House and return to the pub.

PLACES OF INTEREST NEARBY
Only a few miles north are two special attractions. *Steamtown*, at Carnforth, is an excellent railway museum housed on the site of the old railway sheds which closed in 1968 (telephone: 01524 734220). A little further is the *RSPB Leighton Moss Visitor Centre and Reserve* (GR 478751), closed Tuesdays, Christmas Day and Boxing Day. The Reserve is especially famous as the home of rare bitterns.

THE LUNE ESTUARY AND SAMBO'S GRAVE

❦

The northern shore of the estuary of the Lune is tucked away but well worth seeking out. Overton village, with its Norman church, and the failed port at Sunderland Point are picturesque places, the salt marshes with their flowers and birds some of the most accessible in the North West, and Sambo's Grave, believed to be that of a heartbroken slave, an especial treat.

The quay at Sunderland Point

The approach to the estuary of the Lune, through the industrialisation which has crept between Lancaster and Morecambe in recent years, is unprepossessing. Those who do not already know the peninsula defining the northern side of the estuary will be pleasantly surprised by the attractiveness of the area. Overton village is especially picturesque with fine old cottages and houses and, detached on the headland, the church with its panoramic views. Cut off by the tide twice a day, the hamlet of Sunderland Point is a unique part of Lancashire's entrepreneurial heritage which preserves something of a grand failure.

The Globe Hotel is the last building before the sea bank at the bottom of Overton village street. Well into the 1900s, the area immediately behind it was laid out as a pleasure garden to attract visitors from nearby Morecambe. A good menu is on offer from 12 noon to 2 pm and 6.30 pm to 8.30 pm daily; there is a special children's selection. There is an international touch to the choice including, unusually, a Balti dish for vegetarians. Those who prefer more traditional English fare are also well catered for. Together with Mitchell's own ales (including Lancaster Bomber) are Castlemaine and Carling Export lagers, Guinness stout, and Scrumpy Jack cider. The bar is open all day, every day, from 12 noon to 11 pm (10.30 pm on Sunday). Inside there is a non-smoking area and a very pleasant conservatory in which families are especially welcome. The terrace is an attractive spot to sit on sunny days and there is a play area for the children. Dogs are welcome outside.

Telephone: 01524 858228.

- **HOW TO GET THERE:** From the A589 Lancaster to Morecambe road turn for Heysham port opposite the College. Take the turn off the roundabout for Middleton and Overton beyond the industrial estate. Alternatively, approach from the southern end of Morecambe via Heysham and Middleton. There is a passenger rail service to Morecambe. Stagecoach buses run to Overton from Morecambe.
- **PARKING:** Car parking is available at the pub and close by just over the sea bank; there is a little across the marsh at Sunderland Point, and some more at Potts Corner.
- **LENGTH OF THE WALK:** 4 miles; add a mile for the extended route. Map: OS Pathfinder 659 Galgate and Dolphinholme (GR 433579).

THE WALK

1. The first section of this walk crosses the salt marsh which fills the embayment between Sunderland Point and Bazil Point. This area becomes flooded at high tide and so it cannot be undertaken then. You can check the high tide time with Morecambe Information Centre (telephone: 01524 582808) and then allow at least an hour either side of that time. There are also notices about tide times for

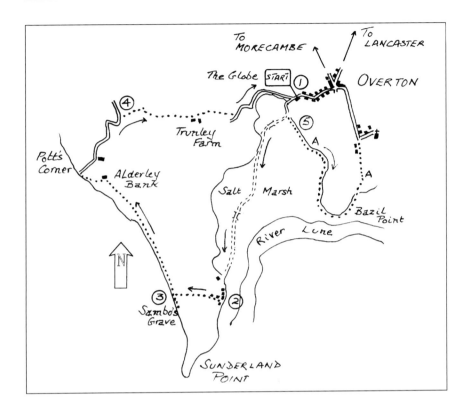

drivers at the car park near the start of the walk. If you get your timing slightly wrong, then it may simply mean a longer stay at The Globe! Turn from the pub towards the sea bank and cross the cattle grid to pass the small informal car park on the shore. Follow the unfenced lane across the grazed marsh. Birds cry and wheel overhead; curlew, lapwing, oystercatcher, and redshank, and many others. Late in the summer sea asters and thrift turn the edges of the sea-weedy gutters into a bright painted blaze of colour.

Once across the marsh it is worth while wandering along the shore at Sunderland Point village. Built in 1728 by Robert Lawson, a Lancaster merchant, who thought Lancaster itself too inconvenient as a port, the quay, the ball-topped gate posts, and some of the houses remain.

2. Turn right across the peninsular along The Lane. Beyond the little mission church, this becomes narrow and overgrown with elder and thorn, but opens out as you reach the far side where the sandstone walls grow blackberries, gorse and harebell. Beyond the gate to the shore go left for 50 yards and back over the wall to Sambo's Grave. Reputedly that of a slave who died of heartbreak on these foreign shores in 1736 when he believed himself abandoned by a beloved master, the grave is never without flowers.

3. Return to the end of The Lane and continue northwards along the top of the shore. Continue along the bottom of the newer section of bank and pass by the house at Alderley Bank along a wettish section. At Pott's Corner you can join the track beside the Shorefields car park and reach the end of Carr Lane, which leads to Middleton village and Heysham. Walk along the lane past Hawthorne House farm on the right, and Middle Brows on the left; the view ahead is of the Ashton Memorial in Williamson Park, in Lancaster. Round the last of a series of bends a footpath leads off into the fields on the right.

4. Use the white up-and-over stile by a reedy drain and go to a second up-and-over stile at a gate. Bear left and right along the hedge to another up-and-over stile and a footpath sign marked 'Trailhome Road'. Walk along the right-hand fence to a stile by an iron gate. Aim left of the buildings of Trunley Farm over the rise to the stile by an iron gate. Bear right to a stile in the field corner and cross the far field to a white up-and-over stile onto the lane. Middleton village lies across the fields to the left. Turn left to return to the start along the inner side of the sea bank.

5. A pleasant addition to the walk, if you have time, is to make it a figure of eight (the route marked A on the sketch map). Cross back over the sea bank to the car park and walk round the shore of Bazil Point, going up by the cottages to St Helen's church. The view across the estuary is worth the detour. Return to the village along the surfaced lane and bear left past cottages dated 1674 to reach The Globe once more.

PLACES OF INTEREST NEARBY
The seaside resort of *Morecambe* is full of interest. It is a post-railway development of 1850 and later.

WALK 3

BY CROOK O'LUNE AND BROOKHOUSE

The views up the Lune valley in this area have been, deservedly, famous for over 200 years. The walk along the river bank can provide a wide variety of bird life and has the unexpected fun of stepping stones and a ford. Settled since at least Roman times, Brookhouse and Caton villages have old and attractive corners.

The 17th-century inn at Caton

Below Caton, the valley narrows towards the sea and above it the river meanders at a lower level through an extensive flood plain. Brookhouse village sits on the higher slopes and links to Caton on the lowest flood-free bench, strung out along the main road. Here, in the 18th century, a series of mills used the waters of the Artle and Forge Becks from the Bowland Fells to the south.

On the southern side of the road about 200 yards west of the roundabout, stands the Ship Inn — so named because the nearby mills made cloth for sails. Built about 1680, the ceilings of the Ship are still low-beamed and a friendly fire blazes in an open hearth. Thwaites beers form the main bar offering, together with Carlsberg and Carling lagers, Guinness stout, and Scrumpy Jack and Woodpecker ciders. Bar times are 11.30 am to 3 pm and 6.30 pm to 11 pm except on Sunday when it is open all day. Food is served from 11.30 am to 2 pm and from 6.30 pm to 9 pm as well as all day on Sunday between 12 noon and 9 pm. You might well have expected Morecambe Bay shrimps on the menu in this area but black pudding with cream and mustard sauce makes a special treat of a traditional northern delicacy. Vegetarians are catered for and there is a special children's menu. Inside is an area for non-smokers and outside a beer garden. Dogs are not permitted inside.

Telephone: 01524 770265.

- **HOW TO GET THERE:** Turn from the M6 junction 34 on the A683 towards Kirkby Lonsdale; the pub is on the right near the centre of the village. Buses are MTL (Heysham) Ltd, Kirkby Lonsdale Mini Coaches, and Stagecoach.
- **PARKING:** Some parking is available at the pub (please ask) and there is a small amount of public parking round the corner by the post office; additional parking is available at Bull Beck and Crook o'Lune Picnic Sites.
- **LENGTH OF THE WALK:** 4½ miles; the alternative route shortens the walk by about a mile. Map: OS Outdoor Leisure 41 Forest of Bowland & Ribblesdale (GR 531646).

THE WALK

1. Leave the pub door and cross the road to look at The Cottage (1693). Walk to the right as far as the roundabout and turn left down Station Road towards the river (there is some car parking on the left here). Walk directly ahead past the RC church to the bed of the old 'Little' North Western Railway, now a walk and cycle way to Lancaster. Built in 1846, to link to the Carlisle line at Hellifield, it closed to passengers in 1954 and to goods in 1966. Turn left and continue along behind the houses under the regrowth of trees and over the bridge crossing the lane to Low Mill. Beyond this are open fields and the views up and across the valley begin to open up. Go on to the old bridge over the Lune at least as far as the view up river. (At the far end, and up the steps, is the Crook o'Lune Picnic

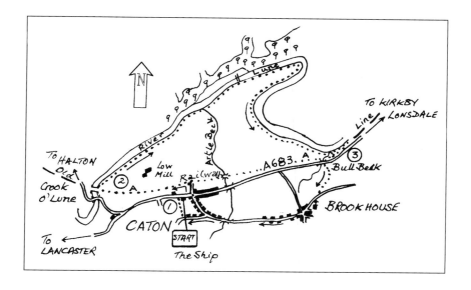

Site with toilets, refreshments, and parking.) It was from roughly this point that John Constable painted the distant view to Ingleborough in 1815, and which shows the field to the left that still cuts down into the woods.

Note: The route described below in point 2 is one used regularly by local walkers, but the riverside portion described becomes impassable when the river floods after heavy rain. Flood conditions are rare but if they preclude you continuing along the riverside, then use the old railway line to walk back to the village and continue (marked 'A' on the sketch map) through to opposite Bull Beck Picnic Site, arriving at point 3 of the walk.

2. Return to the Caton end of the old railway bridge and go right into the field by the river. Drop down to the bottom and use the stile onto the river bank itself. When the water is low enough, the footpath is accessible by jumping the little beck and walking back under the railway bridge. Continue along the river bank upstream now. Across to your right Low Mill, built in 1783, is now converted to other uses, including a trout farm in the former mill lodge, the tumbling outfall of which you pass.

Willows and alders are scattered along the river, and a more or less resident flock of Canada geese should be visible somewhere near the water. The woodlands on the far side have been on these steep banks for centuries; beyond the far bend they are, in part, nature reserve. Eventually you reach the mouth of the Artle Beck with a fine set of stepping stones. BEWARE here at flood times; they may not be passable. The path runs just right of the pseudo-castellated end of the aqueduct bridge.

Pass a second fisherman's hut and the river bends round almost 180° until you will find yourself looking down-valley to the narrows below Crook o'Lune, but walking upstream! Follow the bank round a second bend and ford the Bull Beck (once again it may be difficult after heavy rain). Find the stile up by the old railway wall and work up to rejoin the old track bed. Turn towards the village back across Bull Beck and walk under the trees until almost opposite the entrance of Bull Beck Picnic Site (also with toilets, refreshments and parking). Cross over the main road with care.

3. Go a little left to the footpath up the field. At the top it is worth a final glance back to the meanders of the river. After a stile and an iron kissing gate, join the lane and go right and left to St Paul's church. The old doorway in the west wall depicts the Garden of Eden and a veteran yew stands in the churchyard. The view from down the street, amongst the old stone houses, is a delightfully good one.

Make your way downhill, past the Black Bull Inn, and over the beck. Modern houses infill on the left and then comes the Brookhouse Methodist church. Beyond the Artle Beck bridge, cross over the road opposite the Baptist church. Pass the earlier infill of villas of 1890 and bear to the left along Copy Lane by the bus shelter. A footpath goes to the right opposite Fell View and leads you past old stone cottages and Greenfield to reach the pub again beside the stream, where it looks as though the village washday took place in the past.

PLACES OF INTEREST NEARBY
Lancaster city is but 5 Roman miles away (a milestone was found in the village to record that fact). A few Roman remains, the Priory (founded in 1094 and with the church still in use), a castle (mainly of around 1400) also still used, and a collection of attractive Georgian and Victorian buildings make it well worth while visiting.

ON THE EDGE OF THE HILLS

An easy route through the fields and woods of the Wyre valley beside the river and lakes, with excellent opportunities to glimpse the wildlife. There are some fine views of the western escarpment of the Forest of Bowland. Approaches to the pretty village of Scorton are via winding and narrow lanes from all directions.

The Priory, Scorton

Of all Lancashire's rivers, those which drain the Bowland fells are notorious for the severity of the flash floods which pour from the hills after heavy rain or with melting winter snows. As a result, the shallow valley of the River Wyre north of Garstang has received considerable deposits of workable gravels and the course of the river is now punctuated by a whole series of man-made lakes. Set back from the flood plain is the village of Scorton, a very popular day and weekend visitor venue on the fringe of the Forest of Bowland. Prettily gathered around the offset crossroads, Scorton (with nearby Calder Vale and Dolphinholme) was one of the early industrial hamlets owned by Quaker families who did not permit the sale of intoxicating liquor. Until the 1970s there were no licensed premises here. This explains why The Priory, right in the centre, is not a run-of-the-mill pub but a bar and restaurant.

There is an especially wide menu available at The Priory including, if you have need of it, all-day breakfast. That Lancashire delicacy, cheese and onion pie is listed as an 'old favourite'. Salads, sandwiches and jacket potatoes offer a wide range of fillings for lighter eating. Afternoon teas are something of a speciality. Children are catered for and there is a family area inside. Beer is Thwaites bitter, lager is Carling, stout is Guinness, and cider Strongbow. The bar is open each day from 12 noon to 11 pm (10.30 pm on Sunday). Tables outside provide for fine days. Please ask before taking your dog inside.

Telephone: 01524 791255.

- **HOW TO GET THERE:** Scorton is signed from the A6 at several places north of Garstang on the way from the M6 junction 33; The Priory is at the crossroads in the centre. The nearest station is in Lancaster. From here Stagecoach and Redline buses run to Garstang and there is a local daily Stagecoach service up to Scorton.
- **PARKING:** Behind The Priory and on the wide embayment of the road at the crossroads or at the Scorton Picnic Site at Cleveley Bridge.
- **LENGTH OF THE WALK:** 4 miles. Map: OS Outdoor Leisure 41 Forest of Bowland & Ribblesdale (GR 502488).

THE WALK

1. Go down to the crossroads and turn north on the road signed for Lancaster. About 200 yards beyond the last of the houses turn down left on the Wyre Way footpath sign. Cross the footbridge over the Park Brook and skirt the house gardens with a view out across Scorton Lake to your left. Go back over the brook on a grassed stone bridge, over the stile and left to the footbridge by the tractor ford. Keep ahead between the trees and the corrugated barn and walk along the old bank with rushy fields on the right (with nesting curlew), and the tall heads of yellow flag, and reeds in the silted deep channel on the left. After two fields walk between fences beside marshy ground with ragged robin in season to reach a stile onto a good track. Turn to the right and follow the course of the

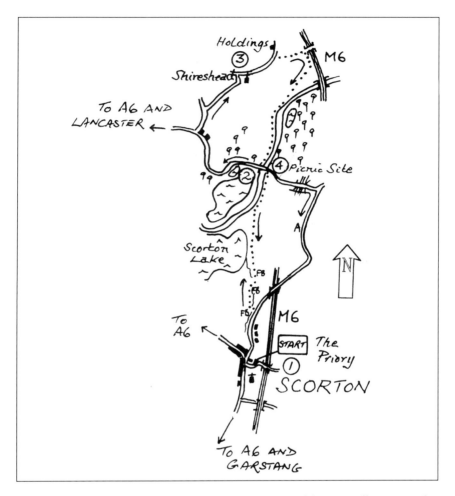

River Wyre upstream; here and there it is possible to walk up on the flood bank. A stile exits to the lane by Cleveley Bridge (reconstructed after the floods of 1953). Across the way and right is the Scorton Picnic Site. A board by the car park entrance gives details of the nature trail and information about wildlife to be seen.

2. Turn to the left on the lane over the bridge. It is pleasant to lean and watch the swift water of the river below; the Wyre here remains a hill river and has not reached the quiet meanderings of the plain to the sea. Continue along the lane past the fine lily pond on the left

23

and round the bend. Climb the brow out of the shallow valley using the right-hand carriageway of the road island (take care for oncoming traffic here and in the narrow section beyond). At the top the view opens out with the tower of Forton Service Station (on the M6) in the near distance and the fells of upper Wyresdale beyond — the ridge from Clougha Pike through Ward Stone makes the skyline. Walk ahead to the junction with Miller Brow beyond Cleveley House Farm and turn right. Go right at the fork in the lane and underneath the power lines to old Shirehead church at the next corner. Gates give access to the graveyard and you can cut the corner by walking through. Abandoned and neglected now, St Paul's dates from 1801.

3. Go along the lane to the right now until just short of The Holdings. A path leads right through a squeeze stile at the far end of the beech hedge. Aim half left towards the end of the footbridge over the M6 with the view of the cairn on Nicky Nook on the hill behind the village ahead. There is no need to cross the footbridge (but you might want to spend a smug minute or two watching the world rush by beneath it!); join the Wyre Way again and go right along the motorway boundary fence. Drop down the field to a stile by a steel gate and cross the largish ditch over a culvert. Follow the water flow into the narrow end of the field between the trees and enter the woodland at a stile by the steel gate. Bluebell, dog's mercury, ramsons, and ragged robin bloom in the dappled shade. Steps lead up onto the embankment and the path follows the treed river bank downstream past gravel banks and rapids and with yellow broom and wild raspberries for the picking.

4. At the laneside turn left back over Cleveley Bridge. Either return the way you came across the fields or continue ahead over the motorway bridge and bear right at the junction to reach the village again by the Lancaster lane (marked A on the sketch map).

PLACES OF INTEREST NEARBY
The nearby little market town of *Garstang*, and its outlier of Churchtown (once upon a day it was the other way round), are delightful. The remains of Greenhalgh castle stand in the fields just outside the town. St Helen's church, at Churchtown, is one of the oldest and most interesting in the county.

WALK 5

A WALK ABOVE THE SALT

The Wyre, Lancashire's third largest estuary in terms of size has, like the Lune to the north and the Ribble to the south, a fascinating richness of wildlife. Man has lived in and cultivated the surrounding marshlands for 2,000 years, at least. Only relatively recently was it realised that the salty marshes hid beneath them a much older and greater treasure hoard of salt. This is a gentle walk with only a minor height rise and with wide views.

The Saracen's Head, Preesall

The phrase 'below the salt' used to signify one's lowly place in society. Here, beside the estuary of the Wyre, everyone is 'above the salt' for the whole area sits over beds of salt some 210 million years old which have brought major industry to the opposite shore. On the eastern side — for the river flows north into the Irish Sea here — embankments prevent tidal flooding of the flat fields and the areas high enough to escape the tides have evidence of a long occupation.

The Saracen's Head stands on the western side of the B5377 in the middle of Preesall village. A carved stone head — said to be the Saracen himself, but looking more like a Roman god — presides over the upper car park of the pub. All the traditional fare is on the menu plus a variety of more international dishes, particularly curries. Vegetarian dishes are available and there is a children's menu. Food is served from 12 noon to 2 pm and between 5.30 pm and 9.30 pm, and all day on both Saturday and Sunday. The bar opens at 12 noon until 3 pm, between 5.30 pm and 11 pm and all day at weekends (10.30 pm Sunday). Beers are Thwaites, the lager is Carling, and the cider Woodpecker. There is a non-smoking area inside and a beer garden. Dogs are not permitted inside.

Telephone: 01253 810346.

- **HOW TO GET THERE:** Use the A588 from Lancaster via Cockerham or from the A586 (from the A6 south of Garstang) via Hambleton and continue on the B5377 towards Knott End west of Stalmine. The nearest stations are Poulton le Fylde and Blackpool (via the Fleetwood ferry). Stagecoach and Harry's buses link Knott End and Poulton.
- **PARKING:** At the pub — but please ask in the bar first.
- **LENGTH OF THE WALK:** 4½ miles with two shorter alternatives available. Map: OS Pathfinder 658 Fleetwood (GR 366473).

THE WALK

1. From the front door of the Saracen's Head it is worth crossing the road for a glance at The Round House, at the bottom of Smithy Lane, and to turn to view the facade of the pub, built around 1820. Return with care for the traffic and go down Back Lane past both old and new brick-built houses until the fork at Town Foot. Bear right along Acres Lane. Move out onto the flatter land by the estuary past Whiteside Cottage (1810) with a temperature gauge built in the wall. Join the footpath along the farm track and walk past the car parks of the Alkali Angling Club. Swing right round the large pond across the field; Preesall village is in view on the ridge. At the sign, continue ahead for Curwen's Hill with a view of the Bowland Fells in the distance to the right. Pheasant and partridge feed on the gleanings of the fields in early autumn. The path leads up the yard right of the house (1735) to a stile to a small field. Leave this by an iron kissing gate in the left-hand corner.

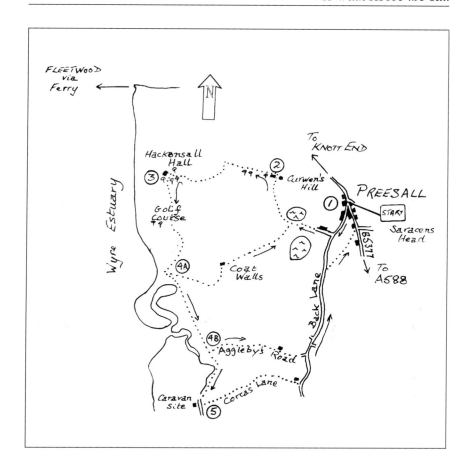

2. Go left now on a grassy track by a wood and beside one field on the left; English oak, with its stalked acorns, grows on the bank. At the end of the field Knott End village is visible across to the right. Turn left along the unmade Whinny Lane with honeysuckle in its hedges: at the next belt of trees pass a pond on the right. The view back shows the relative smallness of the fields around Preesall which indicate its earlier settlement than these flat lands. Continue ahead towards the trees around the renovated Hackensall Hall. The name goes back at least to the reign of King John when Geoffrey the Arblaster received this land for his services though the present building is basically Georgian, at the earliest.

The carved stone head in the pub car park

3. Turn to the left on the track and cross the golf course fairway (take care!). Roman coins have been found here, and down by the shore are traces of old iron smelting sites so the Wyre estuary shore has a long history of human use. The chimney of the ICI works, at Stanah on the far shore, gradually appears to rise out of the top of the sea bank as the track slowly rises. At the next sign, beside the power lines, on top of the bank, take the stile into Barnaby's Sands Nature Reserve (Lancashire Wildlife Trust) and follow the Wyre Way along the bank above the salt marsh and the flotsam of high winter tides. It's worth carrying binoculars for this section of the walk alone. Birdwatching is practicable all the way to The Heads caravan site at Corcas Lane. The view from the bank is extensive and, on clear days, should include Parlick, standing out on the south west corner of Bowland, and Black Combe, in the southern Lake District.

4. Two opportunities exist for shorter circuits. The first (marked A on the sketch map) bears off left at the stile onto the marsh bank and returns via Coat Wells Farm and Acre Lane. The second leaves by a stile to Aggleby's road two-thirds of the way along the bank — the 'Private' sign refers to the land not the path — and exits to Back Lane (marked B on the sketch map).

5. Go left on the bridleway of Corcas Lane and pass a notice which reads 'Preesall Brine Fields'. In fact, you have been circuiting round and through the brine well area since leaving Acre Lane. The deposits below your boots are actually of rock salt and, since about 1870, water has been pumped down into the beds to dissolve it to form the brine which returns to the well heads — most are now enclosed in small brick-walled enclosures scattered across the fields; a few metal structures are still visible — and is pumped across the estuary to the ICI works. In the past some of the rock salt was also mined for export. Pass the brick workshop building and join the tarmac access road to the junction with Back Lane by Corcas Farm. Turn left and cross Grange Pool by a low, white-railinged bridge and continue along Back Lane rising slowly towards the village. Continue straight ahead at Cemetery Lane and pass the ICI Pumping Station with the stump of the old windmill behind it. Just before the houses a track leads off right — there is no sign — and leads up the slope beneath crab apples to reach the main road opposite Park Lane. Turn left and make your way back to the start with care for traffic at the narrow section in the village.

PLACES OF INTEREST NEARBY
Fleetwood, the Victorian port and resort, is accessible by the ferry from Knott End. This operates from May to October but does vary with tide and weather so it is sensible to check beforehand (telephone: 01253 771175) — otherwise you must drive or bus round the estuary. *The Fleetwood Museum* (telephone: 01253 876621) tells the story of the sea and the fishing fleet which have had such a central influence upon the town's history and character; at Farmer Parr's, on Fleetwood Road (telephone: 01253 874389) is a country life museum and animal world. The 'Jacinta', a fishing trawler, can be visited at the Freeport Shopping and Leisure Village (telephone: 01253 878158).

WALK 6

A DAGGER AMONGST THE WILLOWS

The edge of the Fylde plain has many scattered settlements which, like Salwick, don't really have any centre. In the past, the area was of major importance but it is quietly agricultural now with the traffic on the Lancaster canal for pleasure only. The walk is an easy circuit with a richness of wildlife, good views, and opportunity for quiet contemplation.

The Lancaster Canal at Salwick

The countryside north west of Preston has been rich agricultural land for centuries. Tucked in between the poorer hills eastward and the former wetlands of the Fylde, this area of low undulating country shows its history on today's map in the pattern of small irregular fields spattered with a multitude of small ponds, contrasting with the much more recent drained areas with large fields. Much of the present population commutes to work in and around Preston

30

and the M55 sweeps masses of traffic through from the M6 to Blackpool but the former artery of the Lancaster canal has, itself, now been absorbed into the landscape.

Once known as the Clifton Arms, the Hand and Dagger, beside Salwick Bridge, has served travellers since the early 1800s at least. It used to be a regular stop for barges on the canal and, even today, the canal bed regularly gives up lumps of coal unintentionally left behind. A 'Pig and Chicken' Foodhouse menu is on offer here all day, each day from noon until 9 pm (with snacks available between noon and 3 pm — except Sunday). There is a good selection (and, yes, you can have steak if you want it!). Salads cater for the lighter eater and there are both a children's menu and specials of the day for vegetarians. The bar is open all day, every day, from noon. Beers are Greenall's bitter and Caffrey's Irish ale, with Castlemaine, Carling and Stella Artois lagers, Murphy's stout and Strongbow cider. There is both a beer garden and a garden area for children. Please ask before taking your dog inside.

Telephone: 01772 690306.

- **HOW TO GET THERE:** Turn through Clifton off the A583 Preston to Kirkham road or head south from Inskip on the B5269 past the old airfield. There is a station (serving the large works) at Salwick. Redline Travel operates buses out of Preston.
- **PARKING:** At the pub (please ask at the bar).
- **LENGTH OF THE WALK:** 3½ miles; shorter routes of 3 miles and 1½ miles are possible. Map: OS Pathfinder 679 Preston (North) and Kirkham (Lancs) (GR 463330).

THE WALK

1. Cross Treales Road and go down the steps to the towpath of the Lancaster canal to the far side of the bridge. The smart old-style signpost indicates the Preston terminus to be 4¾ miles. Take this direction and go immediately beneath the aqueduct pipes; along this stretch you will probably find pleasure narrow boats moored. The canal sides are rich in wild flowers — red campion, herb robert, roses, and honeysuckle — and the wide variety of trees still includes the sallows (goat willow) from which Salwick derives its name. Swing round the bend of the cutting, past the old canal yard with Salwick Hall in the trees to the left. Once the home of the Cliftons (in former times both doughty soldiers and a law unto themselves —

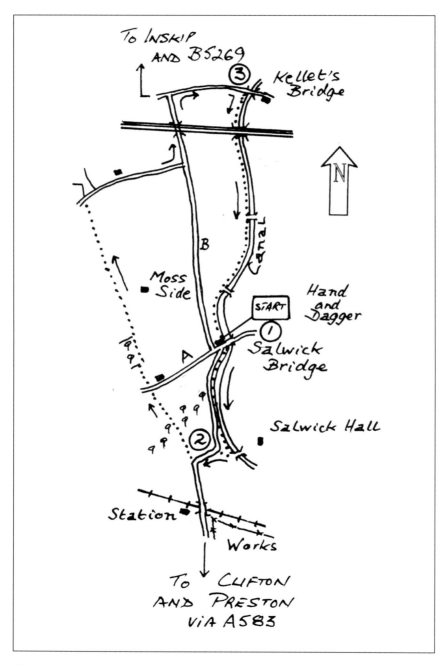

the hand and dagger seems a more than suitable emblem for them!) the remains of the old moat still exist, but it is private and not open to view. At the stone arch of the bridge climb the steps and exit right to the lane.

2. Walk left along the footway to the next bend and go right on the footpath across the field towards the trees. A stile gives access to a narrow belt of beech, sycamore and elm; cross the footbridge and reach the stile to the far field. Walk along the hedge to the road just west of the farm. (You can return direct to the pub from here if you wish, marked A on the sketch map.) Cross over and pass the garden and tennis court on the right. Make for the corner of the wood and walk along with the trees on your left. Pheasants are reared here and it is a veritable warren of rabbits. Away to the right are the fells of the Forest of Bowland with Beacon Fell, its top crowned with dark conifers, in the nearer distance. At the far end go through the gate and continue on the same line parallel to the hedge. Clumps of hawthorn and willow surround the pond to the left: a glance at the map will show that this whole countryside is closely dotted with similar field ponds, often home to moorhen and coot. Pass Moss Side Farm to the right and cross the muddy ditch to walk along the right-hand hedge. Turn to the right along the lane past a plantation of beech and larch and continue past Stanley Grange. Way in the distance is the characteristic bulk of Pendle Hill and far to the north the Lakeland Fells. At the T-junction go left and across the motorway. Drop to a second T-junction and walk right along the lane to Kellet's Bridge with Moss Farm on the other side.

3. Drop right, back onto the towpath by the canal. Occasional fishermen sit quietly waiting most days of the week; yellow flag, cow parsley and meadowsweet decorate the banks. Pass, first, New Bridge and then an old milestone which records 'Preston 6' and 'Garstang 11' — the next bridge (where there is no way off) is, indeed, named Six Mile Bridge. By now you are back amongst trees.

PLACES OF INTEREST NEARBY
You are within easy reach of *Preston*, with the opportunity to visit the *Lancashire Museum*, in Stanley Street (telephone: 01772 264075) with its story of the Red Rose county.

WHERE ASLAND AND RIBBLE MEET

Everywhere here the landscape is wide — sky, marsh, and estuary combine in broad brush strokes with the wind to blow the cobwebs off! Even if you are not much of a birdwatcher, the large numbers of birds which gather to feed on the tide are impressive to see. The walk is flat and a couple of very short circuits are possible.

The Dolphin Inn, Longton

Both sides of the Ribble estuary, though especially the southern side, are lined with vast areas of salt marsh. Now the port of Preston is closed and the main channel is no longer kept clear for shipping, the importance of the area to the county is in the intensive cropping of the reclaimed land behind the long sea banks and the attraction of the marshes to countless wildfowl and waders. Although most of the area is designated for conservation in one form or another some is still shot over during the season. The River Douglas (or Asland) joins the Ribble between Hesketh Bank and Longton and a small pleasure boating business still continues on its banks. Eastward, the marshes are quiet again and left to the grazing beasts and the birds.

The Dolphin (there are, incidentally, two on the sign, rather than one) is located beside the marshes and popular with shooters and fishermen — it is, locally, often referred to as 'The Flying Fish'. It underwent complete refurbishment in 1998 and will take time to fully develop its potential. A Whitbread house with Boddingtons and Whitbread beers, they also serve Heineken and Stella Artois lager, Guinness stout, and Strongbow cider. Bar times are 12 noon to 11 pm Monday to Saturday and 10 am to 10 pm on Sunday. The menu includes stomach-warming meat and potato pies, hot pot, and Butter Pie (potatoes cooked in butter), peas and gravy. A selection of sandwiches and toasties provides good snacks — a Sunday speciality is egg and bacon butties. Food is available all day. There is a family area inside, open fires, and a play area outside for the children as well as a beer garden. Dogs are welcome.

Telephone: 01772 612032.

- **HOW TO GET THERE:** Turn off the A59 on any of the signs for Longton and take Marsh Lane from the right-angled bend in the centre of the village.
- **PARKING:** At the pub.
- **LENGTH OF THE WALK:** 4 miles; 2 or 1½ miles by the shorter routes. Map: OS Pathfinder 688 Preston (South) & Leyland (GR 458254).

THE WALK

1. Take the track northwards immediately beside the pub and pass to the right of the clay pigeon shoot in the first field. Follow the arrowed path on the old bank close to the right-hand boundary to a stile at a fence. Follow the far side of the wire fence now to cross an open field to a gate. Turn to the left on the Ribble Way sign and walk along the sea bank with the vast salt marsh stretching away to your right, with grazing sheep and cattle. Across the river are the buildings of Warton Aerospace factory and downstream the old windmill at Lytham and Blackpool Tower; up the estuary are the West Pennine Moors and the Bowland Fells. Most of the marshland at the mouth of the Ribble is reserve as a consequence of the large flocks of wildfowl and waders which come here, especially in autumn and winter — the best months are September and October. If you time your walk to be a little before high tide (the RSPB

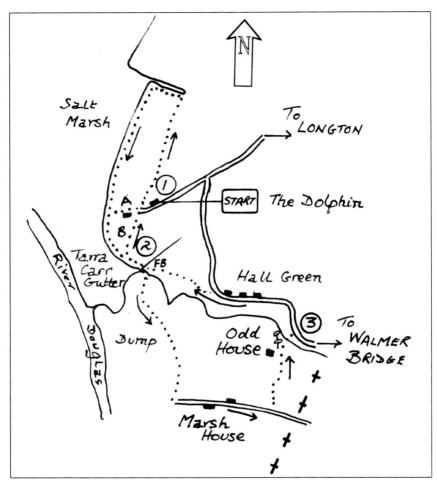

Discovery Centre at Fairhaven Lake, Lytham — telephone: 01253 796292 — will give information, and details of events they organise on both sides of the estuary: they close Monday and Friday during the winter) you would be very unlucky indeed to see nothing of interest as the birds follow the advancing tide across the marsh.

At the first stile on the left you can, if you wish, return the few hundred yards past the bungalow to the pub (marked A on the sketch map). Otherwise, continue along the bank and round the bend to Tarra Carr Gutter. A second quick return opportunity is the stile beside the gate on the left (marked B on the sketch map).

2. Extend the walk by using the stile and footbridge into the field ahead and crossing right over the second stream. There is no footbridge here and the clay banks are steep and can be slippy; so beware of getting wet! The footpath crosses the field on the right-hand boundary to the gate. (When the stream is running high crossing may be impractical.) The sea bank meets the route again at this point. From here you look out to where the River Douglas (or Asland) meets the Ribble. Bear to the left along the fence and join a track which skirts round the edge of the massive man-made mound of the Much Hoole Landfill Site; the arable fields on the left grow corn (maize) as high as the proverbial 'elephant's eye'. Go left along the lane and past a belt of scrubby trees which includes a black poplar. Pass the brick built 'Manor House', dated 1692 over a small window. Walk up the slight rise to the footpath to the left along the access of Odd House Farm; this is before you reach the track of the old railway. Bear to the right off the access track at the sign and pass the farm to the left. Look for the stile on the left by the iron gate. Go over and right on the track to Hall Carr Lane at a copse of beech and oak.

3. Turn left along the lane. Pass the cottages and go round the bend to the hamlet of Hall Green. Just by the next bend, beneath the power lines, a footpath turns off left and follows the old bank top as far as the bend of the stream. This seems to be a favoured spot for herons. At this point, continue straight ahead on the fence line to the footbridge and stile you used at the start of Section 2 of the walk. Use the stile by the gate and follow the fence parallel to the track amongst nettles. Go ahead between fences (with horse boxes and garden on the left) to exit more or less opposite The Dolphin where you began.

PLACES OF INTEREST NEARBY
A little along in the Southport direction from the centre of Longton village is the *Longton Brickcroft Nature Reserve*, off Drumacre Lane. By crossing the River Douglas at Tarleton Bridge and turning right at the traffic lights, you can reach the unique *Lancashire Light Railway* (telephone: 01942 218078). This specialises in 2ft gauge locomotives from quarries and docks.

WALK 8

ANCIENT BORDERLANDS

Before 1974 the great swathe of countryside in the angle of the Hodder and Ribble was in Yorkshire and the Forest of Bowland thereby cut in two. The logical change at that time brought the two Mittons fully together for the first time in at least 800 years. This walk takes you along the Ribble and back to Roman times. There are some wonderful views on offer, too.

Owd Ned's Tavern, Mitton Hall

The Shireburnes, the major landowners of both the Mittons, Great and Little, played the existence of the Lancashire-Yorkshire border, along the Ribble and up the Hodder from the confluence, to their own advantage down the centuries. As you look up from the southern bank of the river it will be obvious why the church and old manor house were built where they still stand and why the Yorkshire Mitton was denominated 'Great'. Only as times became more settled could folk afford to pay less attention to sites with a good all-round view and seek to create more secluded spots.

The Hall at Little Mitton was built by the Shireburnes in about 1500, but was much added to and altered in Victorian times and is surrounded by pleasant gardens and woodland. It promotes itself in a rather unusual way with a restaurant, and overnight 'lodgings', as they quaintly call them, as well as 'Owd Ned's Tavern'. Food is available every day from 11 am to 9 pm with a very extensive menu. There aren't, after all, too many places where you can indulge yourself with a pint tankard of prawns with garlic bread! If you want to be more conventional, how about country broth followed by an excellent grill with Cumberland sausage? Snacks are many — from sandwiches to potato skins or fried cheese and dips. A grand selection of beers is on offer here — Boddingtons bitter and mild, Jennings Cumberland ale, Marstons Pedigree, and Flowers, as well as guest ales. The lagers are Stella Artois and Heineken, and the cider Strongbow and Bulmers. In addition there is a selection of wines from around the world and a good range of malt whiskies. The low-beamed bar with its warming fire and flagged floor is open all day from 11 am to 11 pm (10.30 pm on Sunday). The lounge serves as a family area and there is a large garden. Please ask at the bar before taking your dog inside.

Telephone: 01254 826544.

- **HOW TO GET THERE:** From Whalley use the B6246; from Longridge or Clitheroe use the B6243 and turn on to the B6246. The most convenient stations are Blackburn and Burnley; a limited service may be available to Clitheroe on the Ribble Valley line on summer Sundays. A bus service is operated by Lakelands.
- **PARKING:** There is extensive parking at the Tavern, but please check at the bar.
- **LENGTH OF THE WALK:** 5 miles for both loops, 2½ miles for the Lancashire loop only. Map: OS Outdoor Leisure 41 Forest of Bowland and Ribblesdale (GR 717384).

THE WALK

The walk is in two loops, an Old Yorkshire loop north of the Ribble, and a Lancashire loop south of the Ribble. It is suggested that, even if you decide against the whole of the Yorkshire loop you do cross the river and go as far as the church and back.

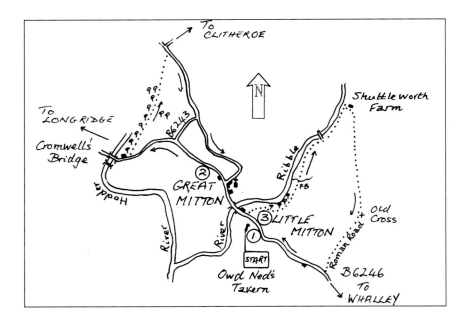

1. Go down to the main entrance, turn left along the footway to pass the Aspinall Arms and cross the river bridge with care for traffic. The bridge parapet still carries the legend 'Little Mitton, Lancashire: Great Mitton, Yorkshire'. Climb up the brow now, under large beeches, and pass the refurbished Manor House on the right. Just around the corner is the entrance to the churchyard. Inside is the interesting Shireburne chapel — though, sadly, you may have to seek the key to see it except around service times.

For the short walk — the Lancashire loop, return to the road and go back over the bridge; further details are given in Section 3 below.

2. For the Yorkshire loop, and the full walk, use the B6246 (which is the Ribble Way at this point) and walk past the Three Fishes pub — itself a venerable building. Continue to the junction with the B6243 and turn left. Walk along as far as the crossing of the River Hodder at Lower Hodder Bridge. On the southern side is the older bridge usually known as 'Cromwell's Bridge'. The structure is actually medieval, but it was here that Oliver Cromwell made the decision to advance along the north bank of the Ribble to cut off the invading Scots at the Battle of Preston. The Hodder is an impressive stream and the view of the three-arched bridge justly famed. Go back up the bank and turn to the left on the footpath beside Moyser Wood. This leads through two fields to New Lane. Turn to the right (on the B6243) and keep left at Mitton Green on the lane which brings you back beside Great Mitton church. Return across the river.

3. On the Clitheroe side of the Aspinall Arms the Ribble Way is signed through a kissing gate. Beyond the buildings Allhallows church and the Manor House become visible on the rise above the far bank. The path follows the top of the eastern bank above the steeply wooded slope, with massive roses and ancient cherries. At a second kissing gate the plantations on the nob end of Longridge Fell are visible to the left. Go over a footbridge and pass the Water Board hut by the weir and the modern arched aqueduct. Leave the Ribble Way at Shuttleworth Farm. The path goes right at the buildings and follows a stoned track which swings back south between the fields and reaches a field gate beside plantings of ash, cherry and oak. Follow the left-hand boundary and continue through at the next gate to a stile in the left-hand corner with the railway line visible two fields away to the left. Cross through the recently planted triangle and jump the ditch to another stile. Walk left through a rushy wet patch to find the obvious base of an old stone cross which sits on the line of the Roman road from Ribchester.

Walk south along the line of the old road (rather indistinct and wet in places) almost to the far end of the field and find stepping stones over a stream and a stile in the bottom left-hand corner. Cross into a now wooded sunken way which leads through to a stile on to the B6246. Cross to the footway on the far side and turn right and walk past the house at Lane Side. Beside the entrance to Little Mitton Hall Farm is a seat on which a small notice records that it was placed here for passing walkers at the bequest of Jessica Lofthouse (to whose books any lover of Lancashire must be greatly indebted!). Complete the loop along the road to the entrance of 'Mitton Hall Lodgings' opposite the kennels.

PLACES OF INTEREST NEARBY
Down the Ribble, at *Ribchester*, are the remains of the Roman fort and an interesting small museum, open all year round (telephone: 01254 878261). Via the B6243 is the market town of *Clitheroe,* with a museum in the former castle of the de Lacy's.

GISBURN AND THE STOCK BECK

The Ribble valley eventually swings away to the north and this point has been a natural crossing of routes down the centuries. Gisburn village has some attractive old buildings. Both the valley of the Stock Beck and that of the Ribble itself have pleasantly wooded sides and there are open views as the walk circuits and returns through Gisburne Park.

A footbridge over the Stock Beck at Crow Park

Since Roman times, and earlier, the road to Yorkshire has headed up the Ribble valley towards the lowest Pennine crossing and through the district of Craven to the great fortress at Skipton and down the River Aire. Our medieval forebears had more concern with the potential of the valley fields and woods and they brought the main route down off the hills which flank Pendle and, where it crosses the road from Burnley to the north, Gisburn village grew to cater for the passer by. Most of the village is widely strung out along the main road and towards the western end stands the Ribblesdale

Arms, once a coaching inn. The continued existence of the large cattle-mart is evidence of the stock-rearing which still continues on the sweet limestone grasslands.

The bar of the Ribblesdale Arms opens at noon and service is all day, every day, until 11 pm (except Sunday; 10.30 pm). Beers are Theakstons bitter and mild and John Smiths, lagers are Fosters, McEwans, and Holsten Export, with Guinness stout, and both Strongbow and Woodpecker ciders. Food is available between 12 noon and 3 pm and from 5 pm to 8.30 pm, and all day on Saturday and Sunday. There are soups, burgers, jacket potatoes, salads and sandwiches. Main meals include some fine home-made pies, and a vegetarian selection. An area inside is reserved for non-smokers, there is a pleasant beer garden, and an unusual play-barn with a witches theme for the children. Dogs are not permitted in the building.

Telephone: 01200 445149.

- **HOW TO GET THERE:** The village of Gisburn lies astride the A59. The nearest station is at Clitheroe; the service is restricted to summer Sundays. ABC Travel operates through buses, which stop at Gisburn and there is a local Lakeland service from Clitheroe.
- **PARKING:** At the pub (please ask), or at the auction mart car park west of the village.
- **LENGTH OF THE WALK:** 3½ miles. Map: OS Outdoor Leisure 41 Forest of Bowland and Ribblesdale (GR 828488).

THE WALK

1. Admire the facade of the pub before you leave, with its coat of arms and date of 1635 over the door: it cost Thomas Lister the princely sum of £855. Walk the length of the street in the Skipton direction. The church of St Mary the Virgin goes back to 1135, or earlier. Inside are four wooden panels bearing the arms of the Listers, Lords Ribblesdale, of Gisburne Park. Through them is a connection with the Pendle witches for it was because Jennet Preston, of Gisburn, was accused of seeking the murder of Martin Lister by witchcraft that she was one of those indicted. Cross over at the corner of the churchyard; by the mini-roundabout a sign on the wall indicates where the Ribble Way turns northwards. Pass out of the eastern end of the village past the vicarage, some modern houses, the Stores and a diner and walk along the wide grass verge

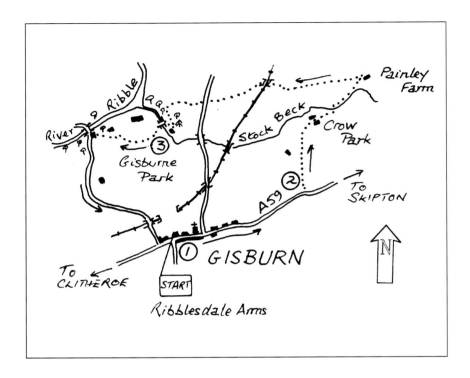

past the derestriction signs. Go round a gentle bend by the Lancashire County Council depot.

2. Bear down to the left at the lane marked as a cul-de-sac and footpath. Pass Deepdale on the left and head towards Crow Park with a view of Ingleborough in the far distance. Go through the yard to the field beyond and drop down towards the Stock Beck on your left. In 200 yards cross the footbridge and bear up the field to the right towards the buildings of Painley Farm. The footpath meets a bridleway at the top of the farm yard. Turn hard left and follow the boundary line past a plantation of Scots pine to the left. Pass the stile and gate and bear right by the bottom of Ha-Ha Hill (could this be so named for the view of Bowland and Pendle — even better from the top no doubt?). Use the steel gate and take the tunnel under the railway line. On the far side the bridleway crosses the shallow valley half left to the stream by a post and a pile of stones. Here I put up a covey of partridge whilst making for the gate to the

A682, with a post dated 1903. Cross direct over the road and walk over the brow to enter the woodland by the stone gate posts. The track drops quickly in a zig zag to Little Painley through a mixture of old oak, beech, hazel and Scots pine and larch. Bear round right to the old stone bridge over the Stock Beck by the pheasant rearing pens. You climb back up the bank now to reach the modern entrance drive to Gisburne Park (now a hospital).

3. Use the wicket gate ahead and swing slowly round on a track with good views of the house frontage to your right. The Listers built this quite pleasant pile, in about 1750, to replace their ancestral home at Westby Hall, off the Burnley road. As you work your way round you cross over the remains of an avenue of lime trees which line the original formal entrance to the Park. Continue through past the horse exercise yard and stables and bear round left. Drop into woods again and go down to the valley of the River Ribble at Gisburn Bridge.

Turn left up Mill Lane beside a tumbling beck through the trees. There is one dramatically twisted beech trunk perched above a small waterfall. At the top of the bank is a group of planted poplars before the bridleway to the right and opposite is the entrance to Deer House Farm close to the outer end of the avenue of limes. Make your way along the lane towards the village. Looking east from the railway bridge you can see the way the railway has been sunk below the parkland of Gisburne Park, and converted into a tunnel with a castellated entrance so that the Ribblesdales would not be disturbed by it — the entrance drive crosses over the top. At the junction with the A59 is the Auction Mart on the right. Turn left at the main road and return to the pub.

PLACES OF INTEREST NEARBY
The road over Gisburn Bridge wanders close by the northern bank of the river for miles. It joins together a chain of attractive villages which can delay you for a long time with ease: Bolton by Bowland, Sawley (with its abbey ruins), Grindleton, West Bradford, and Waddington. North from Bolton by Bowland lie the extensive plantations of *Gisburn Forest* with miles of marked trails and cycleways.

BY YARROW AND LOSTOCK

On a low hillock of dry ground, Croston grew between the Rivers Yarrow and Lostock at the point where together they joined the marshy Douglas valley. Traces of the historic past remain and the walk circles from the old, through the modern, to the minor industrialisation of Victorian times. The rivers flow with lowland placidity and hedgerows and banks flower in profusion in season.

Croston village

Where the flat-flowing Douglas finally ceases to be tidal it is joined by the Yarrow and the Lostock. Here a market grew up probably long before the cross was erected from which Croston takes its name. No doubt the fishermen came up from the sea and in from the marshes and traded their wares with sturdy hill farmers. For a thousand years it was an important place and then sank into relative obscurity until the railway brought minor Victorian industrial development which, in its turn, has faded largely away.

Clustered around the old church is a grouping of buildings of considerable attraction with the Grapes Hotel on its outer edge. Probably dating back 400 years and once serving both as court house and as the lock-up for transgressors who had failed to pay their customs dues on the tidal River Douglas, the Grapes is a welcoming hostelry. Extensive restaurant and bar menus are offered here. Food is not available on Monday but is served from 12 noon to 2 pm and from 5.30 pm to 8 pm (9.30 pm in the restaurant) Tuesday to Friday, and all day at weekends. Vegetarians are well catered for and a children's menu is available. Bar times are 12 noon to 3 pm and 5.30 pm to 11 pm, Tuesday to Friday and 12 noon to 11 pm at the weekend (10.30 pm on Sunday). Beers are Boddingtons, Hartley XB, and Flowers IPA, lagers Heineken and Stella Artois, stout Guinness, and cider Strongbow. Non-smoking and family areas are available inside and there is a beer garden: dogs are not permitted in the building.

Telephone: 01772 600225.

- **HOW TO GET THERE:** Croston village lies on the A581 halfway between the A59 and A49, just west of Chorley. There is a station on the Liverpool to Preston line; bus services are provided by J Fishwick & Sons, P & R Coaches, Redline Travel, and Stagecoach. The Grapes Hotel is at the T-junction just east of the church.
- **PARKING:** At the pub (please ask).
- **LENGTH OF THE WALK:** 3½ miles. Map: OS Pathfinder 699 Chorley & Burscough Bridge (GR 471184).

THE WALK

1. Cross the road to the pretty brick terraces of Church Street, where the old cross stands inset in the cobbles, and walk along to the churchyard of St Michael and All Angels. This has suffered such frequent rebuilding (four times in the 18th century alone!) that its 13th century origins are thoroughly obscured. From some angles the tower appears to lean and the roof spans both nave and aisles. In any case it is but the successor to whatever was established 600 years earlier still by the followers of St Aidan. Backing onto the River Yarrow, the school, founded in 1660 and rebuilt in 1827, is in use yet. On the other side of the churchyard, through the porch, is the old rectory (1722), now a retirement home; the gateway on to the road just north of the pub, is imitation gothic – and seems to have

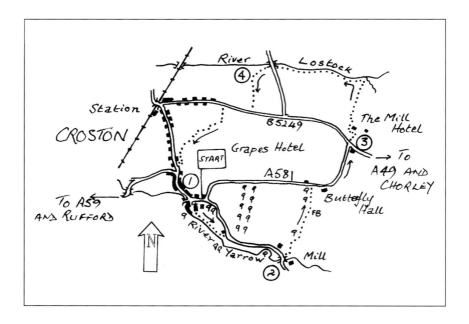

been built to look a ruin. Leave between the church tower and the school (founded in 1660 and rebuilt in 1827), into the trees beside the languid River Yarrow, and go ahead through the modern kissing gate. Follow the field path within sound of coot and moorhen to a stile and sandstone zig-zag squeeze on to Grape Lane. Immediately pass the RC Chapel of the Holy Cross and a little further, on the far side, are the former gates of Croston Hall — now demolished. Continue beside the overgrown shrubbery on the right and along the road lined with limes and elder to reach the river again at a wall on the bend. Go on as far as the near end of Croston Mill bridge; the mill stands on the far bank.

2. Turn to the left on the track away from the river and reach a stile by a gate. Enter the field and look for the step stile and bear to the right, following the arrow, to the shelterbelt of trees. Away to the right, Winter Hill stands out in the distance. The path follows the side of a deep ditch, using a green lane a-hop with rabbits, and with grey squirrels foraging amongst the trees. Keep by the left-hand boundary of two fields, with a footbridge between them, to a stile on to Highfield Road almost opposite a house named Woodlands.

(Hopefully, the notice that 'Dogs not on a lead will be shot' is no more than a variation on 'Please keep your dog on a lead across grazing land'.) Turn right and use the footway — which keeps crossing the road — to join the road junction at The Highfield pub.

3. Cross over and follow the footpath sign along the entrance drive to Gradwell Farm and, in 20 yards, go left into the car park of The Mill Hotel. Walk to the far side and up the side of the buildings to the left-hand corner of the rear car park where there is a gap in the fence and the path crosses to a track. Walk along this past isolated oak and ash to a gate. The line of the path runs over the field in front to the obvious board on the far side. At the board go left on the path (not crossing the footbridge over the side stream) and almost immediately walk beside the main stream of the River Lostock; a favourite haunt of herons. A decayed old bridge and stile lead you across a drainage ditch and the path continues to Littlewood Bridge. Cross immediately over Ridley Lane.

4. Bear half left to find a stile at the junction of hedges and follow the hedge line on the far side to a stile to the footway along the B5249. Turn to the right for about 100 yards and find a footpath to the left before the speed limit signs. Follow the gravel path between fences and hedges to a T-junction and bear to the right behind the houses. At the tarmac road, go immediately left over a footbridge and up-and-over stile and cross the field to another footbridge. Go right to zig zag under overgrown hedges behind the gardens and emerge onto the sports field and play area behind a school. Exit on to the street at the left of the school buildings. Walk left past the almshouses (1692) and keep along Town Road. Here you are in the newer part of Croston, formed around mills, brickworks and the railway in the 1800s. Cross over and walk beside the Yarrow for the final few yards to the Town Bridge (1682) at The Hillocks. The Grapes is over the road at the next corner.

PLACES OF INTEREST NEARBY
To the east is *Astley Hall*, at Chorley. This combines interesting local collections and an art gallery with the house and parkland (telephone: 01257 262166). To the west is the fine partly half-timbered *Rufford Old Hall*, a National Trust house, beside the A59 (telephone: 01704 821254).

WALK 11

BESIDE WINDMILL AND CROSS

The twin villages of Parbold and Newburgh are the first on the plain which extends west towards the sea and is, in the main, fertile arable land. The one was a minor industrial centre in Georgian and Victorian times, and the other remained stubbornly rural. The very easy walk links two Conservation Areas by using the towpath of the Leeds and Liverpool canal.

The Windmill pub, Parbold

If you can, come to Parbold down the hill. The road falls over the red sandstone escarpment beside the Wiggin Tree restaurant into the gap cut by the River Douglas. From this point the view over the richly-agricultural south west Lancashire plain and across Liverpool Bay to North Wales is exceptionally fine. The time is not long past when a score of windmills would have been in the foreground of the view. Today most are gone and even what were once substantial stone towers have usually disappeared amongst the nettles. Modern re-use has saved the one in Parbold village.

Lying on the Southport to Wigan railway line, Parbold is a commuter village now, but there is some substantial evidence of its more recent past in the Conservation Area centred around the canal bridge. The Windmill pub has been serving travellers by road, canal, and then rail for over 200 years. A Greenalls house, they serve their own bitter and mild, as well as Theakstons ales. Lagers are Labatts and Carlings, stout is Murphy's and cider is Strongbow. The bar is open between 11 am and 3 pm and from 5.30 pm to 11 pm (10.30 pm on Sunday). The menu includes the fascinating, and unusual starter of a 'Bloomin' Onion' in batter, and the leg of lamb is justifiably popular. Food service times are 12 noon to 2.15 pm and 6.30 pm to 9.15 pm Monday to Friday, 12 noon to 2.30 pm and 5.30 pm to 9.15 pm on Saturday, and all day on Sunday. Inside there is a family area; there is a play area for the children in the village. Please ask before taking your dog inside.

Telephone: 01257 462935.

- **HOW TO GET THERE:** Use the A6209 from Burscough Bridge or the M6 junction 27 and turn north into the village just west of the traffic lights at the canal bridge Parbold has a station on the Southport to Wigan line. Bus services are by North Western Road Car Co.
- **PARKING:** At the pub (please ask — space is limited), or the public car park on the far side of the canal bridge.
- **LENGTH OF THE WALK:** 2¹/₂ miles; 1¹/₂ miles by the shorter route. Map: OS Pathfinder 699 Chorley and Burscough Bridge (GR 491104).

THE WALK

1. From the front of the pub, turn towards the windmill tower (which is now part of the display space of a home furnishing store). Walk between the tower and the wall onto the canal bank to go along to the aqueduct over the River Douglas at the white painted wooden rails. At the steps up the bank on the left the path leads across the open field to join the main road opposite Greenhill Farm. Up on the hill in front is Beacon Hill Country Park, and Parbold village lies behind with its two churches. Though both churches are Victorian, Parbold is thought to be one of the earliest Christian sites in Lancashire. Perhaps because it was just where the hill lands finally give way to the coastal plain.

2. You are now on the edge of Newburgh village — also a

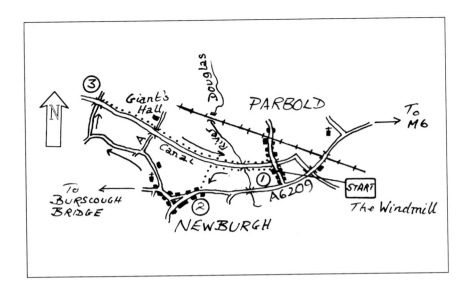

Conservation Area — which, despite the main route through the middle of it, has managed to retain a distinctive character of its own. Cross the main road with care and walk right along the footway. Pass the saddler's and some fine brick houses beyond the Red Lion Inn, which are dated 1691. Keep left along Cobbs Brow Lane, beside the pretty green with its beech trees by the seat and the stone cross. The cottage next to it has edge-set flag stones as a fence. Continue ten yards more and go to the right down Smithy Brow. Cross back over the main road to the corner of Back Lane with its neat post office on the other corner. Follow Back Lane past Christ Church. Ignore the path to the right and continue past the school on the left and the stone farmhouse on the right (1740) and on beyond Culvert Lane. (You could choose to shorten the circuit here; marked A on the sketch map.) Pass the poultry processing plant and the white cottages to reach a tree nursery on the left. Turn right down Deans Lane and drop down by the modern sewage works to go beneath the canal. The aqueduct clearance is only 7ft 3 inches, and a raised walkway saves you getting your feet wet in the puddles which collect on the old flags on the bottom.

3. At the far side of the tunnel, go up to the left by the cottages and join the towpath to make your way back towards the village. There is a fine view of the break in the escarpment made by the Douglas valley, and of the sharp drop along to the north. Road, canal, and railway have all made use of this gap. The ridge of red sandstone is the source of much of the decorative stone in south Lancashire from quarries such as those on Parbold Hill. You soon pass the oblong monolith of Giant's Hall (1679) beside Culvert Lane once again. Continue on the towpath beside hedges and alders to cross back over the River Douglas and reach the car park by the canal bridge. Parbold is where the Leeds and Liverpool canal was linked to the Douglas Navigation in 1772 and this resulted in minor industrialisation for a time. Beyond the bridge stands the former Ainscough flour mill. Once upon a time this was busy enough to have its own fleet of barges on the canal. Turn back over the bridge to reach the pub.

PLACES OF INTEREST NEARBY
On the far side of Burscough Bridge is the *Wild Fowl Trust Centre* at Martin Mere. Not only are there more than 120 species of waterfowl from all over the world kept in the gardens, but vast numbers of migrant birds — especially geese — appear on the re-created mere in the winter. Telephone: 01704 895181.

BENEATH WINTER HILL

The bulk of Winter Hill is familiar to everyone using the south Lancashire motorways. At its foot lie the Rivington and Anglezarke reservoirs and these, and the surrounding area, are justifiably popular for walking. The contrasts of hill, woodland and water make the landscape always attractive and the wildlife varied.

Upper Rivington reservoir

When I ask southerner friends when they feel they have reached the 'real' North the answer always seems to be 'when we see Winter Hill'. Even those who walk not a single step, if they can help it, on Lancashire's hallowed ground, can pick out its great bulk with its skyward TV mast on top as they drive the M6 or M61, and the way in which it catches the first dusting of snow is a salutary reminder of the turn of the seasons. Wide and soggy grass moorlands stretch in all directions and then, on its western edge, give way to the man-made delights of the Rivington and Anglezarke reservoirs: not all of man's efforts turn out to be destructive of landscape.

On the corner of the delightfully named Babylon Lane from Adlington, where it meets the right-angled bend of Long Lane from Chorley, by the duck pond, is the three-storey Bay Horse pub. Built about 1750, parts of the buildings are listed; the restaurant was once the smithy and the low beams and both open fire and wood-burning stove make for a welcoming atmosphere. Beers, here, are Greenalls bitter and mild, Bass, Toby Light, Caffrey's Irish Ale, and Worthington's Creamflow; the stout is Guinness, and the cider Strongbow. The bar is open all day, every day, from 12 noon to 11 pm (10.30 pm on Sunday). Food is served between 12 noon and 2.30 pm and 6 pm and 9 pm (not Monday evening), and 12 noon to 7 pm on Sunday. The mixed grills and Sunday three-course roast lunches are especially popular with the locals. Families are welcomed in the TV room and there is a garden area; the restaurant is a non-smoking area. Behind the pub is a bowling club with a crown green. Please ask before taking your dog inside. Telephone: 01257 480309.

- **HOW TO GET THERE:** From the A673, in the centre of Adlington, take the Rivington road; the Bay Horse is at the junction with the Limbrick and Chorley lane just before the bridge over the M61. Alternatively, turn at The Millstone off the A673, just past the Lower Rivington reservoir dam, about half way between Horwich and Adlington, and pass Headless Cross, towards Rivington and then Chorley. There is a station in Adlington. Blue Bus Coaches run from Adlington or Chorley.
- **PARKING:** There is a large car park at the pub.
- **LENGTH OF THE WALK:** 3½ miles. Map: OS Explorer 19 West Pennine Moors (GR 612145).

THE WALK

1. On the right-hand verge, across from the pub doorway, is an 'Adlington Way' sign. Follow the sign towards the motorway bridge and walk across and bear to the right on the footway along New Lane. Pass some brick houses and stone cottages on the left and turn left along the track. Half right is Winter Hill, with the woodlands of Rivington Park and Gardens on its lower flanks — and half left is the skyline of Redmond's Edge and Great Hill above Anglezarke Moor with the gash of Lead Mines Clough running back eastwards. No one seems to have had much success with the mines here.

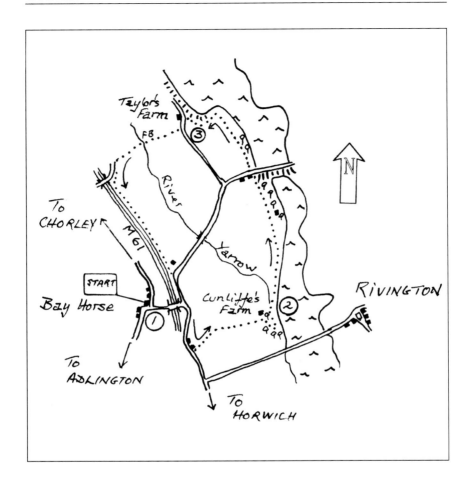

Proceed between the stone wall and the hedge to a stile into a field and follow along the right-hand boundary. A first glimpse of the Upper and Lower Rivington Reservoirs, built to supply Liverpool in the 1850s, appears in the valley below. Pass a cattle trough and, at the next gate, go ahead past Cunliffe's Farm using the stile to the right and the path by the hedge to a stile onto the entrance track. Then walk to the lane which runs beside the reservoir.

2. Turn to the left beneath the beech trees on a small cliff and arrive at a reedy bay where the River Yarrow flows out of the reservoir. The Dovecote at the top corner of Rivington Gardens stands out.

Continue beside fields for a short while and then enter the trees once more near the house called The Street. On the left-hand bank, hidden amongst the foliage, where squirrels forage, is the gravestone of much-loved dogs Sam, and Laddie, and Thomas, the cat. Pass a couple of stone cottages and exit by the Lodge and Knowsley Farm, by a white wooden gate, onto the lane to Rivington village over the dam of the highest, Anglezarke, reservoir. Continue directly across and along the right-hand boundary of the field beside the wall (the dip of the ground is often rather wet). The path traverses a more heathy, open bank above the reservoir, with the old quarries and Anglezarke picnic site across on the far side. Follow the yellow arrow round to the left and go right around the retaining embankment to reach the corner of Charnock Back Lane at a steel gate.

3. Bear left and pass Taylors Farm (1719) between high hedges of holly. In 100 yards, go to the right on the bridleway beside the stone barn and drop down the wooded ravine by the stream to a footbridge and ford of the River Yarrow. Rise up the far side amongst the trees to the entrance of Old Stone Heath Court. Turn left on the lane for 20 yards and find a footpath left into the field. Follow the right-hand boundary down towards the M61 and follow the hedge through a series of fields to reach the lane of Nickleton Brow just right of the detached house. Walk ahead to join New Lane again and cross back right over the motorway to the start at the Bay Horse.

PLACES OF INTEREST NEARBY
On the far side of the Lower Rivington reservoir are the pretty village of *Rivington* and *Rivington Country Park* — originally donated to the public by Lord Lever in 1902. Here, at Great Barn, is one of the finest cruck-built barns to be seen anywhere, and an information centre. Close by is the Georgian-fronted Rivington Hall. Slightly further towards Horwich are Rivington Gardens, now restored and with a wide variety of pleasant walks. Immediately behind them is the detached hill of Rivington Pike with its folly tower. Down below is the replica of Liverpool castle beside the reservoir.

NABS HEAD AND THE BOTTOMS

The valleys of the River Darwen and its tributary, the Arley Brook, are surprisingly dramatic where they slice into the broad bench on the south side of the Ribble Valley. The woodlands are charming at all seasons, but especially so in autumn and winter. Past industry has faded into the background and the hamlets in the Bottoms are very attractive indeed.

The River Darwen at Samlesbury Bottoms

The modern parish of Samlesbury doesn't have a village in a 'gathered together' sense. The folk who lived with Samel — a thousand years ago — settled by the ford over the River Ribble (today just east of the M6 crossing) but the Lords of the Manor moved to a safer site after the havoc wreaked by the Scots in 1322, and Nabs Head and Samlesbury Bottoms appear to be the product of the Industrial Revolution.

What is now the Nabs Head pub was originally built as a house by Thomas Shorrock, who built the mill in the Bottoms, and the pub occupied the house next door. Sometime in the early part of this century, the two buildings swopped uses. Today, the Victorian magnate's home makes a welcoming hostelry. Food is served from 12 noon to 2.30 pm (except Monday) and between 5.30 pm and 8.30 pm. The standard menu is a simple one but does include the rather rare offering of a Barnsley lamb chop (that's the double chop!) and some excellent home-made soups. The children have their own choice and, indeed, families are especially welcomed here. The speciality is summer barbecues outdoors. There is a small beer garden and the village play area is just along the road. Bar times are 12 noon to 3 pm and 5.30 pm to 11 pm (10.30 pm on Sunday). Thwaites beers are on tap, together with Carling, Carlsberg and Warsteiner lagers, Guinness stout, and Strongbow cider. Dogs are not permitted in the building.

Telephone: 01254 852455.

- **HOW TO GET THERE:** Either, turn into Nabs Head Lane off the A677 just to the west of Samlesbury Hall (not far from the M6 junction 31), or turn off the A675 at the Boar's Head, Hoghton, and follow the signs through. The nearest practicable stations for most people will be Preston or Blackburn; the station at Pleasington is just possible if you have the time to make the walk longer (see end of Walk directions for your route). Stagecoach and Redline Travel buses run on the A672.
- **PARKING:** At the Nabs Head (please ask).
- **LENGTH OF THE WALK:** 4 miles; the additional walk from Pleasington station adds 1½ miles one way. Map: OS Explorer 19 West Pennine Moors (GR 622292).

THE WALK

1. Leave the car park and turn to the right down Goosefoot Lane. The lane descends quickly, past Lakeside Lodge (take care for traffic on the bends), to the old mill at Samlesbury Bottoms. Across the bridge over the Darwen the path leads off upstream to the left at the first bend. The small field on the left has been laid out as a recreation area for local people to use and a permitted path crosses it to join the footpath at the far corner beside the weir.

Follow the clear track by the river through the fields with fine broadleaved woodland on the far bank. At the end of the large field you cross into Hoghton parish. Over the stile, bear up the track to

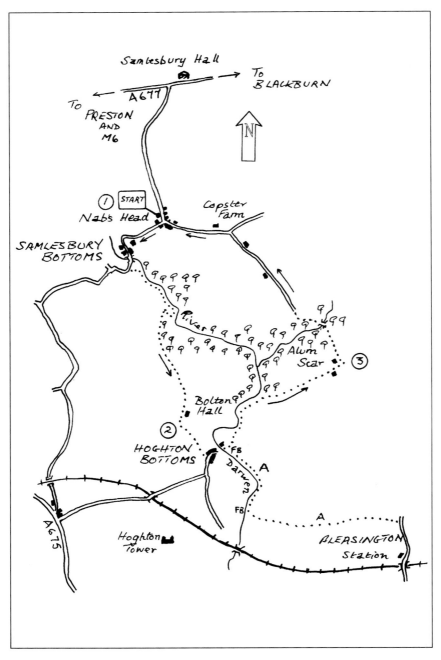

the right. Bend left up the slope and cross the field to the top left-hand corner by the wooded bank above the river. Follow the boundary of Wildbottoms Wood along the top of the steep slope. Ahead is the large wooded knoll on which stands Hoghton Tower and behind the view is across to Fairsnape in the Bowland Fells. Eventually reach a stile by a gate with square stone posts. Follow the track right of the broken wall across the fields towards Bolton Hall farm. On the distant skyline, Darwen Tower stands. Pass the buildings on the left to join the access track and look for the stile to the left just past the entrance to Highfield Farm.

2. Go steeply down the field beneath the telephone line and drop into the bottom right-hand corner through gorse and scrub. A stile leads to a path behind Tallentine Farm and a second stile which exits onto the lane by Grassdale Cottage. Walk left through the stone cottages of Hoghton Bottoms. Cross back over the river at the far end on a green steel footbridge and go straight through the garden of Lower Park Farm on the 'Witton Weavers Way' sign. Pick up the track downstream and pass a fishermen's hut on the right.

The track now climbs the valley side amongst some fine beech trees and rises and swings away from the river; squirrels seem to love this bank. There is an especially good view through the wooded cleft in late autumn and winter. Just beyond the obvious viewpoint a stream crosses the track. Turn up this on the nearside and cross the stream amongst scrub a little before the wall. A stile gives access to a field. Follow the old hedge line towards Close Farm and go through by the gate onto a road end beside the entrance to Alum Scar.

3. Round the high wall of the garden go left by the iron rails and drop down through Alum Scar Wood. The old cobbled track descends through woods filled with heaps of spoil and dark pools: remnants of the former alum mines, the alum being used as a mordant for dyes. By the stone bridge at the bottom, where you move back into Samlesbury, the Arley Brook tumbles over rock beds in small waterfalls. Beneath the big beech tree the beds of shale from which the alum was extracted are exposed. Climb up out of the valley once again and reach the corner of a lane. Continue ahead to the junction with Further Lane. Turn left past Copster Farm and return to the Nabs Head.

Walkers using Pleasington station: Instead of going downstream at Lower Park Farm (section 2), another branch of the 'Witton Weavers Way' follows the river bank upstream to a second footbridge. The path off left, uphill past the golf course, leads into Pleasington village, with the station about ¼ mile along to the right. (Marked A on the sketch map.)

PLACES OF INTEREST NEARBY

Samlesbury Hall lies just on the Blackburn side of the junction of Nabs Head Lane with the A677. In addition to viewing the Hall and wooded grounds, antiques sales are held from time to time (telephone: 01254 812010). In the other direction is *Hoghton Tower*, just off the A675. The long-held belief that Shakespeare was amongst a company of players here has recently received expert support (telephone: 01254 852986).

RODDLESWORTH AND TOCKHOLES

This fine walk up the valley of the Roddlesworth Brook includes both the pleasant waterside of the reservoirs and mid-Lancashire's most extensive area of broadleaved woodland. There are good views up to the Darwen Moors and across the Ribble Valley. The scattered community of Tockholes has a long history and some fascinating old farm buildings and contrasts with the Victorian industrial creation of Abbey Village.

The Hare & Hounds, Abbey Village

The plainly industrial Abbey Village pops up, almost out of the blue, for the traveller along the old Bolton to Preston turnpike road. It is strung out along the roadside for perhaps a mile altogether in a sequence of practical Victorian stone terraces which its inhabitants make some considerable effort in trying to beautify. It forms a conveniently accessible base for exploring the valley of the Roddlesworth Brook.

The Hare & Hounds is the last building at the southern end of the village. The bar is open from 12 noon to 2.30 pm and from 5 pm to 11 pm Monday to Friday and all day at weekends (to 10.30 pm on Sunday). Beers are Whitbreads with Boddingtons bitter, Timothy Taylor Landlord, Flowers IPA, a mild, and guest ales. Lagers are Stella Artois and Heineken, stouts are both Murphy's and Guinness, and cider is Strongbow. Food is served from 12 noon to 2.30 pm and between 5 pm and 8.30 pm Monday to Friday, and between 12 noon and 8 pm on Saturday and Sunday. The speciality here is curry on a Friday evening — including a vegetarian one. More traditional offerings on the menu include gammon, steaks, roast beef and fish; the cheese and onion pie is made with fresh cream. Children are welcomed and have their own menu to choose from: dogs are welcome too! On sunny summer days tables on the forecourt enable you to watch the world rushing by as you relax.

Telephone: 01254 830334.

- **HOW TO GET THERE:** Abbey Village lies astride the A675 a couple of miles south of the M65 junction 3. The starting point is at the southern end of the street at the junction of the Bolton Road and Dole Lane (signed to Withnell). Nearest convenient stations are Chorley and Blackburn. Stagecoach buses serve Abbey Village: Darwen Coach Services and White Lady Coaches serve Tockholes.
- **PARKING:** At the Hare & Hounds or, if you wish to make the pub half way in your walk, at the car park on the Tockholes lane at Ryal Fold.
- **LENGTH OF THE WALK:** 4 miles: starting from Ryal Fold adds rather less than a mile. Map: OS Explorer 19 West Pennine Moors (GR 643224).

THE WALK

1. Start the walk along the surfaced track at the south end of the pub car park past the 'Roddlesworth Reservoirs' sign. This leads along the top of the dam of Rake Brook reservoir, which is steeply stepped down into the valley on the left. Directly ahead Darwen Tower, built to commemorate Queen Victoria's Diamond Jubilee in 1897, stands out on the ridge of the moor. Turn to the left down the steps just before the house and bear left beside the ford to the footbridge over the massive spillway. Go over the bridge and amongst shrubbery and rhododendron to the sign at the end of the dam of Lower Roddlesworth reservoir.

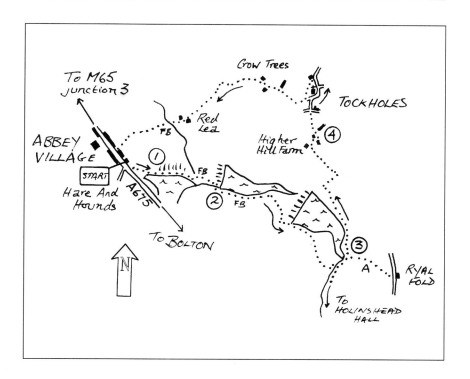

2. Cross the footbridge to the right on the 'Woods and Water' trail and go left along the reservoir shore beside a small group of pines and amongst brackeny mixed woodland of beech, alder, birch, willow, and oak. Pass over a small footbridge and through the wall and climb up amongst tall, columnar beech and sycamore. At the meeting of the tracks, keep straight ahead on the surfaced track past the Water Board maintenance hut. Continue on, past the end of the dam of Higher Roddlesworth reservoir, on a path layered with bark chippings. The path rises slowly up through the woods and then drops down to the Roddlesworth Brook as it comes tumbling down over beds of sandstone. Cross the flat bridge to the left and turn downstream. Work around the wet patch by the trail post close to the wall and find a second sign at the wall end.

From this post it is possible to walk up the bank through the wood to the car park and seasonal Information Centre beside the Royal Arms at Ryal Fold (marked A on the sketch map) and to make the pub the mid-point of the walk.

3. Stay with the trails to continue to the left down the valley beside the reed beds and move into the pine plantations. At a post marked for the 'Nature Trail', beside a seat, go down into the side valley, over a footbridge, and up the steps. Climb the bank amongst broadleaved trees once more to join a track at a large steel culvert pipe. Bear to the left and eventually walk amongst pines again. At the next white footpath marker stay on the track up the slope and contour along the top of the wood to the footpath to the right through the kissing gate into a field. Move up the field on the old green track to a heap of flag stones. Turn left on a cross-path which runs below a pond and along the old boundary ditch towards the buildings of Higher Hill Farm. Bear to the right to a stone squeeze stile by the gate onto the access track. The farm is unusual in having a stone garderobe (toilet) cantilevered out at first floor level. Down to the left you can see across the valley to the reservoirs below and the village of Withnell on the far ridge.

4. Go right up the track to the junction by Rose Cottage and turn left. Immediately bear down to the left (before the stone terrace) and follow the sunken bridleway to the crossroads at the junction with the lane at Lower Hill. Walk ahead on Chapels Lane and swing right round Tockholes United Reformed church with its odd table-like gravestones on decorative pilasters. At the end of the field on the left, double back through the kissing gate at Lodge Farm and cross the triangular field to a gate by the graveyard wall. Bear half right to a stone stile into the farmyard. Walk through to the lane and turn to the right. Follow down past high hedges of holly and elder to pass the end of the row of cottages known as Engine Brow (where once a winding engine for the Lower Mill stood). On the left is a stone drinking trough and then Higher Crow Trees Farm. Continue down the yard to leave Lower Crow Trees on your right and exit to a field — these buildings, and many others you pass, being 17th century or even earlier. The path bears off left to run down beside the stream to a gate at the bottom left-hand. Turn to the left on the far side and immediately cross the old ford and continue on the old bank and track to Red Lea.

The path goes to the right round the far side of the buildings and drops sharply down the bank to stone steps and a footbridge over the Roddlesworth Brook. A stile exits to a track. Almost directly across is a second stile and a set of steps leading steeply up out of the valley again to a stile in the corner of the field by the wood, beside stables. Cross the field and the access track to an old squeeze stile and continue ahead to swing slightly left and come to the Bolton Road in the village between the rows of mill cottages. Just to the right and across is the former mill — now used by a variety of industries and businesses. The village is, in fact, a 'model' village of the 1840s and the mill kept going until 1971. Turn left and walk up the footway to the pub.

PLACES OF INTEREST NEARBY

From the flat bridge just before the end of section 2 of the walk, you can turn up the Roddlesworth Brook and walk to the ruins of *Holinshead Hall* and the well close beside them. As the manor of Tockholes, the site dates back to the 13th century, but the present buildings are essentially 18th-century. There is also a car park on the Tockholes lane at GR 664202.

CHAPELTOWN AND JUMBLES

The walk explores the narrower reaches of the Bradshaw valley, through some fine woodland and beside the pleasant waters of Jumbles reservoir. On the way there is much of industrial, archaeological and historical interest and plenty of wildlife. There is also a chance to visit historic Turton Tower.

Mill cottages in Turton Bottoms

The villages of Chapeltown, Turton Bottoms and Edgeworth, in the middle reaches of the valley of the Bradshaw Brook are an intriguing mixture of 18th-century (and earlier) agricultural communities, built in stone, and Victorian industry — now gone — which used imported brick. The whole valley is yet another in the West Pennines where a series of reservoirs, built to supply Bolton, has completely altered the countryside and where man's modern activities have enhanced a landscape downgraded by his earlier efforts, rather than otherwise.

In the centre of the main village street of Chapeltown stands the Chetham's Arms. The bar is open from 12 noon to 11 pm daily (10.30 pm on Sunday). A wide range of beers is on tap: Boddingtons, Castle Eden, Timothy Taylor's Landlord, Thwaites, Flowers IPA, Chesters Mild, and other guest ales. Stout is Guinness, the lagers Heineken and Stella Artois, and the cider is Strongbow. Both the family and the dog are welcome. You can eat well here from an extensive menu. For the lighter eater there are filled baguettes, sandwiches, and salads. If you fancy something more filling there are few other places in the county with rabbit stew on the menu! There are vegetarian choices too. Food is served from 12 noon to 2 pm and from 5 pm to 10 pm Monday to Thursday, and all day Friday, Saturday and Sunday.

Telephone: 01254 852279.

- **HOW TO GET THERE:** Use the B6391 from Bromley Cross, just north of Bolton, or from the A666 at Bull Hill summit, south of Darwen. Nearest stations are Entwistle (only practicable on foot) or Bromley Cross. Buses are provided by White Lady Coaches or a Stagecoach/ GM Buses North/Timeline joint service.
- **PARKING:** At the pub or, if making the pub your halfway point, at Jumbles Country Park car park (another car park exists at Horrobin Lane).
- **LENGTH OF THE WALK:** 4 miles. Map: OS Explorer 19 West Pennine Moors (GR 733157).

THE WALK

Before moving off, take a few steps left from the door of the Chetham's Arms and have a look at the impressive frontage of Chetham's Farm on the main street; cross over and walk back past the pub so that you get a good view of that building too. The coat of arms above the door, and the date of 1746, put it firmly in context.

1. Walk south along the attractive street of stone cottages and houses to St Anne's, the parish church of Turton (until 1974 an Urban District of Lancashire). An early Victorian edifice on a superbly chosen site, the views from the churchyard are grand. At the far end of the churchyard bear down the bank half left through the up-ended flags and drop to the Edgeworth road. Cross over and

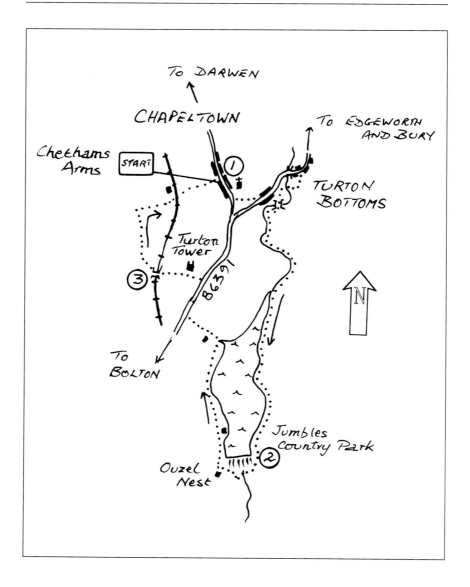

walk along the footway downhill past the imposing brick former Conservative Club of 1904 (now a residential home). Keep ahead beside the railings to cross the bridge over the Bradshaw Brook (widened in 1901) in Turton Bottoms. Go past the Spread Eagle (dated 1851) and turn right into Birches Road to pass the fine row of

Turton Tower

stone cottages. At the fork, go right by No 24 Vale Street and find the path by a small field on the left which leads to a stone footbridge back over the river. Rise up a small brow and turn left on a setted road between houses. Cross the river for a third time beside the stepped weir. Bear immediately right downstream on the river bank and swing round the house and terrace to walk through beautiful woodland in the narrow valley.

Eventually reach the upper end of Jumbles reservoir (constructed as recently as 1971) and follow the track along the near shore. You pass the first twelve posts of a nature trail, for which a leaflet is available at the seasonal Information Centre at the car park and toilets; there is also an open access bird hide off to the left. Below the waters of the reservoir lie the remains of Horrobin Mill (closed in 1941) and there are a few industrial remains along the path. The county boundary crosses the reservoir and, for about a mile, you move outside Lancashire proper.

2. Leave the Information Centre, cross the car park to the bottom right-hand corner and go steeply down the stepped path. Turn right to the footbridge over the brook below the dam and go up a step or two into Ouzel Nest Meadows; an information board about the wildlife is provided by the Croal/Irwell Valley Partnership. Keep steeply up the bank to the right for a short way past a fine oak with a heavily bolled base. A stile in the corner leads into the trees behind the garden of Ouzel Nest. Walk up by the wall and exit onto the unmade road; turn right. The path leads between the tall gateposts of The Grange and bears left beyond the house through the small wicket and between the stables into a field. Cross to a kissing gate and a path beside the willows and alders on the side of the reservoir with fine views up the valley.

At Horrobin Fold there is a sailing club and a bridge over Hazelhurst Brook which comes in from the west. Cross over and go left up the setted Horrobin Lane (the car park is just to the right, the entrance to Horrobin Fold across the clough to the left). The clough itself is a nature reserve. At the B6391 turn right, cross over and walk up the hill to the entrance drive of Turton Tower. Go along the driveway and keep ahead to the battlemented bridge over the railway. Just before this, on the right, is a large water wheel, resited from Black Beck calico printing mill (1830s to 1900).

3. Keep on the track (part of the Witton Weavers Way) and up the wooded clough to the wall. Turn right, away from the small ford, and use the kissing gate onto the track which rises gently beside the field wall. Way to the right, on the far skyline, is the Peel Monument on Holcombe Moor. Pass the old concrete silage clamp and turn down to the right over a stile just past the group of oak and sycamore. An old green track descends beside the clough to a level crossing next to a stone mill with a squat, square stone chimney. Cross over with care and go ahead on the setted lane on an embankment. Fork left up the brow, pass the pub car park, and return to the main street of Chapeltown.

PLACES OF INTEREST NEARBY

Turton Tower is a Lancashire County Museum. Opening hours are complex and it is wise to telephone to check: 01204 852203. Originally a 15th-century defensive tower, the building was modified around 1600.

THE GRANE

A series of three reservoirs now occupies the valley of Haslingden Grane. The walk circuits the middle of the three, the Ogden reservoir. There are wide views of the West Pennine moorlands and an almost continuous reminder of the quarrying and mill working past of the area.

Lower Deep Clough and Ogden reservoir

Changes brought by the completion of the M65, west of Blackburn, and M66, north from Bury, have resulted in the traffic increasing in recent times on the Grane Road from Haslingden to Blackburn. Both commercial and car drivers have, as a consequence, the chance to enjoy some of Lancashire's finest moorland scenery. Stopping and taking a walk around one, or more, of the reservoirs reveals a landscape with history as well as beauty.

The Duke of Wellington pub stands directly at the roadside overlooking the middle, Ogden, reservoir. The bar is open all day, every day from 11 am to 11 pm (10.30 pm on Sunday). Beers here are Boddingtons and Flowers bitters and Chesters mild, the lagers are Heineken and Stella Artois, the stout Murphy's and the cider Strongbow. There is also a good selection of wines on sale by the glass. Food service is from 11 am to 10 pm daily. On offer is the very extensive Brewers Fayre menu and the well-filled car park speaks of satisfied patrons. Vegetarians are very well catered for indeed. There is a good children's choice and this is one of those rare establishments with a Children's Certificate. The fine beer garden looks out straight down the valley. Dogs are not permitted in the building.

Telephone: 01706 215610.

- **HOW TO GET THERE:** The B6232 runs the length of the valley from the junction of the M65 at Blackburn to Haslingden; the Duke of Wellington is about 2 miles from Haslingden town centre. The nearest main line station is Blackburn; East Lancashire Light Railway runs from Bolton Street Station in Bury to Rawtenstall at weekends and on Bank Holidays (telephone: 0161 7647790). Burnley & Pendle Transport and Rossendale Transport run a joint bus service along the Grane road.
- **PARKING:** At the pub (please ask), the Clough Head Information Centre (GR 752232), or Calf Hey (GR 655228).
- **LENGTH OF THE WALK:** 3½ miles. Map: OS Explorer 19 West Pennine Moors (GR 766229).

THE WALK

1. Cross over the road in front of the pub and walk left up a gentle rise to the row of cottages on the right at Heap Clough. Turn right on the quarry road (there is a footpath sign) and go ahead to the bottom of the obvious spoil heaps of the old quarry on the right. Beware of quarry traffic from the still active Jamestone Quarry! Stiles by the two gates both lead on to the track bearing up half left between the boundary fence and the plantation of Scots pine and Japanese larch. Take the fork to the left near the top of the quarry fence — so joining the Rossendale Way — and bear over the rough pasture to descend quickly to the footbridge over the stream in Deep Clough. The path skirts the edge of a small abandoned quarry face and then goes steeply up for a short way to the corner of the Jamestone Quarry fence by a Rossendale Way sign. Continue ahead, outside the quarry fence, and join the old track along the bottom of

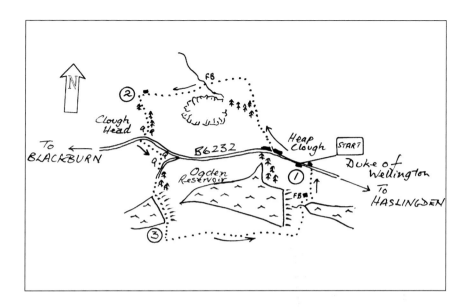

the hillside. Across the valley, to the left, the skyline is irregular with the old workings of the massive quarries which once provided setts, kerbs and flagstones. At the second ruin is a clump of large sycamores which provided shelter to this former farm. Cross the next fence by a stile.

2. Turn down immediately to the left on the footpath (off the Rossendale Way now) and to a stile into young plantations. Continue to a stile on the right: this leads directly into the Clough Head car park. Go straight on and over the field to a stile leading into alders planted on the edge of an old quarry. The path winds through and to the right and emerges into the field again close to the roadside fence. Follow this on the left and cross the stream to a stile onto the verge. Cross over with care and go right for a few yards and then left on the path which follows the stream down towards Calf Hey. You will get a glimpse of the reservoirs lower down the valley through the trees. At the bend of the lane continue ahead on the path marked 'Bird Hide' and go above the beeches to steps to a wicket gate at the edge of the Calf Hey car park. The Grane Chapel stood here from 1815 to 1955 and the graveyard still remains. Follow through the car park and join the lane beyond the far gate to drop to a picnic table overlooking Calf Hey reservoir. Take the gate to the left and go down the slope beside the plantations and pass the preserved 20″ Gate Valve on the left. Walk across the reservoir dam to the gate at the far end, wider here than elsewhere because it had to be reconstructed after slippage took place during the building in 1856.

3. Go immediately left over the stile next to the gate on the far side and up the bank through rushes. On the right is a windblown ash which has begun to grow once again. At the top cross a stile beside an isolated oak and bear left to join the Rossendale Way again. The old track follows the contour amongst bilberry and heather with the Ogden reservoir (1912) below on your left; it was this which closed the cotton mills and led to the depopulation of the valley. Pass some ruined buildings — where there is a good view over the valley to Deep Clough — and bear down to the left at the Rossendale Way sign beside the side stream. Down the valley lie Haslingden and Rawtenstall, and behind is the impressive table top of Cowpe Low.

Descend the valley side to the bottom of the old quarry incline. Beware of the tunnel through the ramp; this looks increasingly dangerous as the years progress and I suggest you divert the few yards round the ramp end to avoid using it. On the far side, go left at the stile in the fence and follow the yellow-topped posts down towards the top of Holden Wood reservoir, leaving Tenements Farm across to your right. Cross over the footbridge — it's worth keeping an eye out for dippers on the outflow from the Ogden dam — and go right along the Water Works wall and left at the up-and-over stile into the field. Walk up quite steeply parallel to the left-hand boundary to reach the road opposite Grane Lodge. Cross over to the footway and walk back 100 yards to the start.

PLACES OF INTEREST NEARBY
Along the B6235, below Holden Wood reservoir, are the fascinating *Textile Museums* at Helmshore (open Easter to October; telephone: 01706 226469). Almost at the turn is the former St Stephen's church, now housing an antiques centre.

HAMLET OF THE SWANS

A close look at the countryside around Altham uncovers some very pleasant corners and links with the past and reveals some of the wildlife which continues to flourish in this part of Lancashire. Views to the surrounding hills are especially good. The walk follows the River Calder for part of the route and then circuits back via the lower valley side.

St James' church, Altham

Between the West Pennine Moors and the ridge which eventually ends in Pendle Hill is the broad trough drained by the River Calder and the Hyndburn Brook. There is plenty of evidence of past industry despite modern changes, and there are still many pleasant spots and good views to be found. Altham village ('the hamlet of the swans') lies strung out by the main road east of the bridge over the Calder.

Right beside the church is the low stone building of the 18th century Walton Arms with flagged floors and oak beams. Unusually, this is a Jennings (Cockermouth) pub and sells their beers and Caffrey's Irish ale. The lagers are Heineken and Stella Artois and the stout Guinness; cider is in bottle only. Bar times are 11.30 am to 3 pm and 5.30 pm to 11 pm; 12 noon to 10.30 pm on Sunday. On offer is a good menu with interesting sea food and fish starters and, for main course, the very popular 'Lamb Jennings' cooked in ale. There is a wide variety of sandwiches, both hot and cold, and salad platters. Vegetarian choices are available. Food service is 12 noon to 2.30 pm and 6 pm to 9.30 pm (10 pm on Saturday), and all day on Sunday. Dogs are not allowed in the building.

Telephone: 01282 774444.

- **HOW TO GET THERE:** Altham is on the A678 Clayton le Moors to Padiham road about 2 miles from the M65 junction 8; from the motorway turn for Padiham on the A6068 and go left at the traffic lights. Nearest stations are Huncoat and Hapton (from the latter of which it is practicable to link to the walk on foot — walk north to the canal bridge, joining the towpath. Go west to cross by Shuttleworth House and join the Burnley Way, under the A6068 and go right to Shuttleworth Hall, Point 3 below). The bus service is provided by Stagecoach.
- **PARKING:** At the pub.
- **LENGTH OF THE WALK:** 2½ miles. Map: OS Explorer 19 West Pennine Moors (GR 771329).

THE WALK

1. Turn to the left from the front of the pub. Walk the 10 yards to the churchyard lych-gate and go down through the trees to the church of St James itself. A panel on the side of the gate records the death of 68 people in the nearby Moorfield colliery disaster of 1883. On the edge of the bench above the flood plain of the river, this remains one of the most delightfully situated and attractive churches in the county, despite the striding pylons and the very visible modern industrial premises. Return from the church to the main road and go left along the footway to the near end of the bridge. A lucky summer's evening may still find those swans on the water below the ancient church. Cross over the main road with care for traffic. Take the lower track by the old mill (there is no sign) and look for the stile onto a green track beside the woodyard — here, unusually, they specialise in processing local hardwood timber. Take the stile to

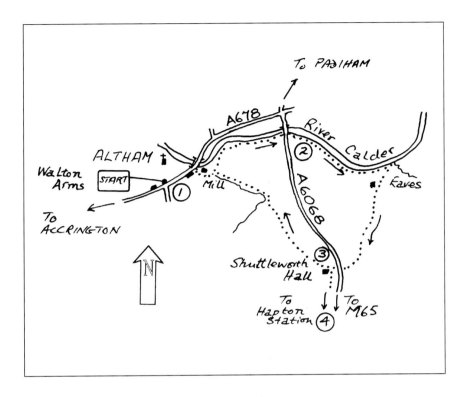

the right into the field beside the pylon, walk along the old steel fence round what appear to be the remains of Second World War buildings and turn up on to the embankment beside the River Calder. Way up the valley, Hameldon Hill dominates the ridge on the Yorkshire border. Continue on the bank, across from the Simonstone industrial park, to pass beneath the modern bridge carrying the A6068.

2. The path goes through recent plantings of alder and willow, remaining beside the river, and swings round a long bend to the next stile. Pass by the end of the double steel bridge, which gives access to the electricity grid distribution station on the far side, and go left over a stile to rejoin the bank once again. Ducks dabble in the shallows and there are clear signs of an old ford at the bottom of a section of stony rapids. The river bends in the other direction now and you walk along beneath the bench on which Eaves Farm stands. Just before reaching the weir, look for the stile in the corner to the right and immediately cross over the farm access lane to a second stile. Here you join the Burnley Way.

Bear slightly right up the slope of the field and aim left of the farm buildings to a stile in the right-hand corner. Aim across the field for the second pylon ahead and cross to a stile beside an oak tree on which there is a square yellow board — and in which I surprised a squirrel hoarding nuts! There is a half-drowned stone over the ditch and you need to angle slightly right towards the nearer pylon to find a stile just to its right. Follow up the hedge line, the view up-valley opening up towards Yorkshire as you rise. Go right at the stile by the gate in the top right-hand corner of the field and follow the right-hand boundary — first a hedge and then a wall, with a view across to Pendle Hill — to the main road. Cross directly over with great care for traffic coming fast from the motorway to your left! Two stiles lead you to the corner of Shuttleworth Hall. This is a fine example of a yeoman's house of the late 1600s with projecting wings and stone mullioned windows.

3. Leave the Burnley Way at this point and go ahead into the farm yard. Bear right to find the track behind the buildings which leads first through funnelling walls and out into fields. The valley lies spread out below, the river snaking away north west towards the wooded gap in the ridge which leads to Whalley, with Longridge Fell and the fells of Bowland beyond. Gradually descend the valley side and, at the bottom, go through the gate and swing left by the stream to a stile and gate. Follow the signs (at the time of writing the footpath was diverted for a short way to avoid the edge of the Altham Industrial Estate development) downstream to the gate in the corner and join a short section of track to the mill. Bear left and return to the main road and walk left to the pub.

PLACES OF INTEREST NEARBY

A couple of miles from the route, at Padiham, is the very fine National Trust property of *Gawthorpe Hall*, with its collections of embroidery, lace and costumes, and pleasant gardens (telephone: 01282 778511).

BY BARLEY WATER AND BLACK MOSS

Since prehistoric times the countryside around Pendle Hill has evoked response from those who live beneath it and travel within sight of it. Things are no different at the turn of the Millennium and this walk from Barley village enables you to pay your homage in any way you will. The valley of the Barley Water is a delight and the open rough grazing over Black Moss a fine foreground to views of Pendle.

Pendle Big End and Upper Black Moss reservoir

The picturesque — no other word will do — village of Barley lies hard under the Big End of Pendle Hill and is deservedly very popular for day outings. The association of Barley, and nearby Roughlee and Newchurch in Pendle, with the Witch Trials of 1612 is well known and has been written about many times so this countryside is often already a familiar one, even to the first-time visitor. Nonetheless, the reality is ever impressive. Somehow the Hill never quite gets around to smiling down on you and, under a towering stormy sky or beneath a blanket of grey winter cloud its great bulk has the effect of mountains many times its size elsewhere.

In the middle of the village, across the lane from the swift Barley Water, is the Pendle Inn. Quite incredibly this is only a 1930s creation, but very sympathetically done with warming open fires in the winter. The bar is open daily from 12 noon to 11 pm (10.30 pm on Sunday). Beers are Greenalls, Tetley and Tapsters Choice bitters and Tetley mild. The lagers are Castlemaine and Carlsberg, the stout Guinness and the cider Strongbow. There is an uncommon speciality in fruit wines. On the menu is a selection of home-made pies and the usual range of meat dishes. Hot and cold sandwiches and filled potatoes are on offer for the snack eater. Vegetarians are catered for, as are the children. Food is available all day in summer, winter times are 12 noon to 3 pm and 6 pm to 10 pm. Inside are family and non-smokers' areas and outside are a beer garden and play area for the children. Dogs are welcome. Accommodation is available.

Telephone: 01282 614808.

- **HOW TO GET THERE:** Approach either from Fence (on the A6068) via Newchurch in Pendle, or from the A682 via Roughlee. Nearest stations are Brierfield and Nelson. Bus services are by Lakeland and the summer weekend 'Pendle Witch Hopper' running between Burnley and Clitheroe.
- **PARKING:** At the Pendle Inn or the public car park (GR 823403).
- **LENGTH OF THE WALK:** 3 miles. Map: OS Outdoor Leisure 41 Forest of Bowland & Ribblesdale (GR 820404).

THE WALK

1. From the front door of the pub use the left-hand entrance to the car park, cross the lane and turn back, downstream, on the path behind the wall and next to the Barley Water. Opposite the pub, cross over on a footbridge and walk through the picnic area to the public car park by the toilets and seasonal Information Centre. Exit from the car park at the bottom right-hand corner on the sign for the 'Pendle Way'. Pick up the track leading to the former Narrowgates cotton spinning mill and cottages. Continue past the cottages and down the river past the old farm, the bridge to the right, and the plantation of pines to the left. At the wooden gate is a

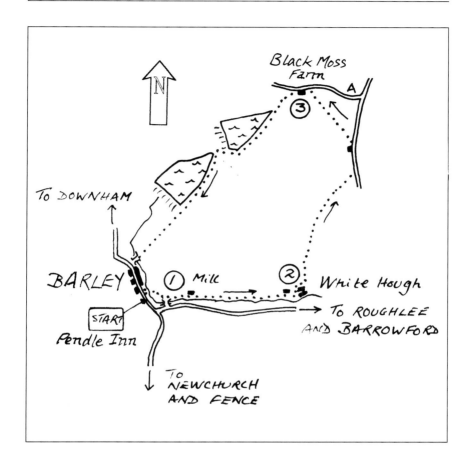

sandstone squeeze stile and a memorial seat overlooking the flowing water. The river bank is wooded with occasional Norway maples on the far side. At the hamlet of White Hough follow through in front of the buildings to the lane to the left between the cottages and walk up past the old farm, with stone mullioned windows and the carved coats of arms — the oldest dated building in the area (1593).

2. Continue to climb up the lane beside the tumbling beck. Ignore the path to the right by the brick hut and go ahead to the Outdoor Pursuits Centre. Go to the right round the end of the buildings before the farm entrance and up the footpath overhung with holly and other trees. At the field boundary there is a stile and a second immediately to the left which leads through new plantings to a stone stile in the wall. Bear slightly right up the slope and find the grooves of an old grassy track to go eventually between wire fences as it begins to flatten out. Reach a lane at a stile. Turn to the left along the lane and drop down just beyond the house to a stile and wicket gate to the left. Cross the garden extension and aim right of the nearest telegraph pole to find a stone stile in the wall. Continue to drop down a very wet and rushy field to the stile by the gate close to Black Moss Farm. As an alternative (marked A on the sketch map), it is possible to continue along the lane and turn first left to avoid the wet patch.

3. Walk to the left and go left again on the footpath just beyond the farm. The Big End of Pendle towers immediately in front of you reflected fitfully in the never-quite-still waters of the reservoir. Cross the field down to an up-and-over stile by a stone barn and go left over the farm bridge and on to the track. Go to the left and walk down the track beside Upper Black Moss reservoir and gently descend. Below the dam, turn to the left and follow the wall of Lower Black Moss reservoir to pass the lower dam and spillway. The reservoirs were originally built between 1894 and 1903 to provide water to the expanding town of Nelson. Continue to join the road at the corner of the village. Walk left, past the Primitive Methodist chapel of 1910 and rows of stone cottages to return to the start.

PLACES OF INTEREST NEARBY
It would be a pity to miss the opportunity to see the delightful Georgian church of St Mary's at *Newchurch in Pendle*. It is Newchurch which has made the most of the tourist potential of the story of the Pendle witches. In Barrowford is the *Pendle Heritage Centre*, on Colne Road. Although the Information Centre is open all year, opening times of the displays are more restricted and it is wise to check first (telephone: 01282 842214).

MERECLOUGH TO CANT CLOUGH

This walk gives a taster of the wild Pennine edge and links some of the more unusual industrial history of the area with what some regard as the most attractive remaining Tudor buildings in all Lancashire. The valley of the Rocky Water is dramatic in its small way and contrasts strongly with the sweeping views above.

Cant Clough reservoir

On the moorland edge, where it rises towards the final Pennine ridge, lie a series of formerly isolated hamlets which, these days, are largely dormitories to Burnley. Of these, Mereclough is the most southerly and is where the old road rises sharply up the moorside to head across towards Todmorden. The modern main road passes straight through towards Holme Chapel and bypasses the old heart of the village.

The Fighting Cocks pub (rebuilt in 1901) dominates the roadside and preserves the memory of bygone sport. Like many other

Greenalls pubs, the Fighting Cocks offers the 'Millers Kitchen' menu. With a good old English focus, it also provides a range of international dishes and an excellent vegetarian choice. As a result, enticing combinations are easy. Food service is all day from 11.30 am to 9.30 pm (from noon on Sunday). Draught beers are Boddingtons, Tetley's and Caffrey's with a guest ale. The lagers are Carling, Carlsberg, and Stella Artois, stout is Murphy's, and cider Strongbow. The bar is open from 11.30 am to 11 pm (10.30 pm on Sunday). Families are especially welcome and there are both garden and inside play areas. Dogs are not permitted in the building.
Telephone: 01282 455069.

- **HOW TO GET THERE:** Use the A646 Burnley to Todmorden road and turn at Walk Mill or Holme Chapel through Over Town. Burnley Central is the nearest convenient station. Calderline and Lakeland provide bus services.
- **PARKING:** Either at the pub or at the Hurstwood picnic site (GR 882312).
- **LENGTH OF THE WALK:** 4 miles. Map: OS Outdoor Leisure 21 South Pennines (GR 873304).

THE WALK

1. Leave the car park and walk to the corner beyond the telephone box. Turn right by the Kettledrum pub (named after a racehorse which won the Derby) on Long Causeway. Take the footpath at the end of Mereclough Barn and cross the garden to a stile into a field. Follow the green track up the shallow depression with a silted pond and oak wood on the far side (could this be what is left of the mere in the clough?). Cross the wall at a stile, follow the left-hand wall up to a stone stile on to a track and turn to the right. The view opens up to Worsthorne Moor and its eroding peat hags, and the old quarries on Pike Stones; over your left shoulder lies the bulk of Pendle Hill. Pass the farm buildings of Brown Hill and turn left down the track between Rosemary Cottage and the entrace to Rock Water Bird Centre (which is open to view between about Easter and October — not Mondays). Drop sharply down the slope and into open woodland in the valley of the Rock Water. The bridleway leads to a stone bridge over the river and sharply, but briefly, up to the attractive stone hamlet of Hurstwood immediately opposite Spenser House (where Edmund Spenser — 1552 to 1599 — author of the

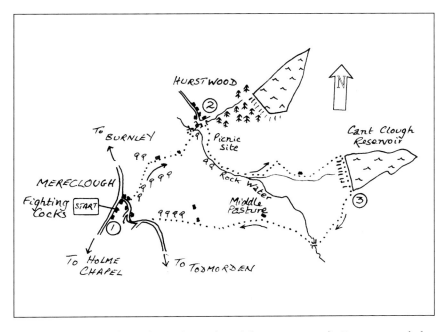

Faerie Queen is thought to have lived for two years). Just around the corner is the fine Hurstwood Hall, dated 1579.

2. Walk past the front of the Hall towards the old red telephone box and cross the bridge over the brook which flows down from Hurstwood reservoir. Go along the track to the picnic site and car park. Turn to the right before the lower gate and drop down the bank to a kissing gate. Follow the path up-valley (ignoring the path to the right over the footbridge) and find a second kissing gate. The valley narrows and you walk below the face of an old quarry, climbing up to the left to look down on the meander of the Rock Water cut deeply into the sandstone beds. At the ruin of Hey Laithe continue straight ahead up the side valley and follow round the corner of the wall to climb up to a stile beside a gate. Turn right on the track to pass the white bungalow. Go through the gate below the water works and up the gently sloping track towards the dam of Cant Clough reservoir. Turn across the dam to the gate at the far end. The upper valley shows the former quarry workings below Hazel Edge.

3. On the skyline ahead is the wind farm on Mosscrop Hill, on the Yorkshire side of the boundary. Follow the track round the bottom of Worsthorne Moor and drop down into Sheddon Clough. The strange and battered landscape above the bridge was created by hushing for blocks of limestone buried in the clay and sand deposits between about 1600 and 1800. Hushing was a method of extracting ores and minerals by damming streams and suddenly releasing the water and so washing away the lighter materials. The bridge itself is built of oddly reddened stone (could these stones have earlier formed part of lime kilns, I wonder?). Once across the stream go right up the bank on the Burnley Way. Over the brow is a kissing gate and some more, outlying workings. At the stile by the next gate bear right past the farm of Middle Pasture.

Level with the far end of the buildings, bear off half left across the rushy rough pasture towards the left-hand corner. Cross a small stream by a culvert and rise to a stile by the gate right in the corner. Follow the boundary wall past modern farm buildings and the older buildings of Near Pasture, off to the right. A stile gives on to the access lane. Walk ahead past the heavily grazed shelterbelt of oak and sycamore and start to drop down. At the T-junction turn to the right and stay with the main road steeply down and around the bends past a house called Deo Favente (behind it is the old graveyard); in the quarry just beyond is a small memorial garden. The lane bends round past cottages dated 1704 and returns to the corner by the Kettledrum pub. Go left to reach the start.

PLACES OF INTEREST NEARBY

A Trail exists through the impressive *Sheddon Clough* (details available from the Information Centre in Burnley) and can be added to the walk. Alternatively, you can use the Long Causeway road to a car park at the top of the clough (GR 891290). The road, of itself, brings exciting pictures of a Bronze Age past to mind. The whole sweep of the moor is open access land on which, if you have the necessary stout boots, rainproof clothing, and know how to use map and compass, you can wander at will.

ABOVE WATERFOOT

The walk is a circuit up the middle reaches of the Irwell Valley and back along the moorland side. Although the valley bottom is well built up — quite often even over the river — there is much of interest from the past to see. Now the old quarries are abandoned, the side cloughs are pleasant and peaceful places.

The Royal Hotel, Waterfoot

The Rossendale Valley is, in fact, the valley of the River Irwell. Although it has been heavily industrialised over 200 years, it is narrow and steep-sided and the bright moorland streams tumble down the cloughs. Even the valley bottom retains a variety of interest and walking part of the Irwell Valley Way is a good way to see it in a detail which travelling the main road by car cannot match. It is in these towns and among these hills that the characters of Edwin Waugh's (1817–1900) dialect poetry took their inspiration and it is here that you'll still find the ghost of the Lancashire dialect he recorded in daily use.

Waterfoot is one of the more distinguishable places along the main road and the Royal Hotel stands turn-of-the-century proud just east of the main junction. Food is served here from 7 am to 3 pm and from 5 pm to 9 pm (except Friday and Saturday evenings). It won't be a surprise that such an early opening hour brings with it a 'Mega' breakfast — three bacon rashers, three eggs, three sausages, plus — certainly an unusual way to start a walk! Snacks include toasted sandwiches, filled jacket potatoes, burgers and pizzas and main meals offer all the usual meats and trimmings; there is a children's menu too. The beers are Theakstons and their own 'Royal Hotel', with Fosters and Becks lagers, Guinness stout, and Strongbow cider. The bar is open all day from 11 am to 11 pm (10.30 pm on Sunday). There is a small beer garden and families are welcome. Please ask before taking your dog inside. Accommodation is available.

Telephone: 01706 214493.

- **HOW TO GET THERE:** On the A681 Rawtenstall to Bacup road. There are no main line stations in the Rossendale valley but it is possible to get to Rawtenstall using the East Lancashire Light Railway from Bolton Street Station in Bury at weekends and on Bank Holidays (telephone: 0161 7647790). Bus services are provided by Rossendale Transport.
- **PARKING:** In the public car parks either behind the Royal Hotel, or across the road (disk only).
- **LENGTH OF THE WALK:** 4 miles. Map: OS Pathfinder 690 Rawtenstall & Hebden Bridge (GR 834217).

THE WALK

Note: It is wise, especially for families, to carry a torch to help keep your feet dry on the walk through the old railway tunnel.

1. Leave the Royal Hotel forecourt to the right and turn right into Cowpe Road in 20 yards. Cross over at the car park entrance in a further 20 yards and take the track on the nearside of the River Irwell — following the sign of a dragonfly for the Irwell Valley Way — and rise up a little next to the coal yard on the left which occupies the site of the former station. At the red steel bridge by the weir go to the left to the main road and turn right on the footway past Glen Terrace and into the entrance of the Thrutch Gorge. Here

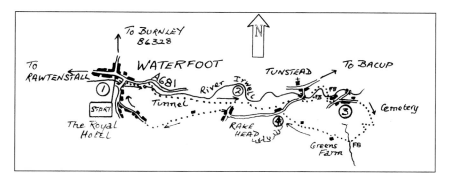

the river cut 120 feet into the thin-bedded sandstones at some time at the end of the last Ice Age. Flowering plants, rhododendrons and the occasional tree cling precariously here and there. Turn to the right on a path which leads on to the bed of the old railway track to Bacup beside a carved pillar in a small formal garden (there is also a footpath sign on a nearby lamp post) and walk into the railway tunnel. Although the surface underfoot is good, the constant drip of drainage water has formed puddles here and there and you are liable to get wet feet without additional light as you traverse the 200 yards below ground. Continue ahead and rise to a gate beside the old bridge.

2. Cross directly over the lane and drop back onto the former railway track past the cricket ground on the left. Rejoin the river now to Atherton Holme Mill. A path bears up to the right to an Irwell Valley sign half way up to a long stone terrace; turn left. Proceed forward to a stile and exit to a lane. Go down the brow to the left to the bridge over the river at Blackwood Road. It is worth a 50 yard diversion to the main road corner to get a closer look at the neat building of Holy Trinity, Tunstead, with its octagonal tower and small spire (1841) and the two old pubs on opposite corners; the Railway Tavern and the Oddfellows Arms.

Take the stile on the side of the bridge away from the main road and walk upstream for 200 yards to a concrete and steel footbridge across the river. The path continues on the river bank around the bend to a kissing gate opposite a recreation ground. Turn right between the fence made of upended flags and the stone wall to another footbridge back across to the south bank of the river, close to the end of an old mill. Bear right up the nearside of the mill and go left on the cobbled lane behind it to exit onto Acre Mill Road. Cross over and use the footway down the hill to the corner of Brunswick Terrace (before the river bridge). Turn right on the sign 'To the Cemetery'.

3. The road leads up to the main cemetery gates; turn to the right just before these beside the monumental mason's workshop, following the Irwell Valley Way. The path leads up the hillside beside old hedges and with small fields bounded by old upended flagstones. At the top, turn left along the lane to the white cottages on the corner at Cutlers Green and go immediately left beside the hens and geese to a stile into a field. An old green track runs along the bottom of the field to the right and descends to a bridge made of massive flagstones over the splashing water of Greens Clough. The track swings up right to a stile and then a gate. Go immediately right to a second gate into the yard of Greens Farm and walk through and ahead past No 6. Take the track to the right which leads gently down (Holy Trinity church should be visible again down in the valley). Use the concessionary path to the right at the steel kissing gate by the white house and walk through to the road.

4. Turn to the left past the terrace of cottages and walk along the road below the large Rakehead Landfill Site in the former quarries. This is slowly being landscaped and reclaimed. At the stone cottages of Rake Head take the right-hand turn. Go round the bends to No 25 and turn to the left along Royds Road. This unmade track leads along first past Royds Farm and then Heys Farm on the right. At the gate and stile, continue ahead by the left-hand boundary and drop down a little to the bottom of the field. Turn right along the nearside of the boundary and join the road at Tenterheads — where finished cloth was once stretched in the sun to bleach. Continue down the hill to reach Cowpe Road via Carr Lane. Cross to beside the rushing stream beneath the small wooded cliff and drop back the few hundred yards to cross the Irwell bridge and bear left through the car park and between the buildings to the starting point.

PLACES OF INTEREST NEARBY

A worthwhile addition to your visit to Rossendale is the *Lambert Howarth Footwear Museum*, open daily except Sunday: turn at the lights in Waterfoot (telephone: 01706 215417).

INFORMATION

Bus Operators

Bus services and timetables are liable to alteration at short notice and walkers are advised to check details with the operators concerned when planning a particular outing.

ABC Travel	01704 576033
Blue Bus Coaches	01204 668112
Burnley & Pendle Transport	01282 425244
Calderline	01422 365985
Darwen Coach Services	01254 776877
J Fishwick & Sons	01772 421207
GM Buses North	0161 627 2929
Harry's	01772 683472
Kirkby Lonsdale Mini Coaches	01524 272239
Lakeland	01254 826646
MTL (Heysham) Ltd	01524 855569
P & R Coaches	01772 312577
Redline Travel	01772 422669
Rossendale Transport	01706 212337
Stagecoach	01772 886633 or 01946 592000
Timeline	01942 680088
White Lady Coaches	01254 771893

So-called 'Rambler' services operate in the Lune valley, the Forest of Bowland and in the West Pennines on summer Sundays and may get you closer to the start of certain walks: enquire at the nearest Information Centre.

RAIL

National Rail Enquiry number 0345 484950. Up-to-date timetabling is available on the Internet at http://www.railtrack.co.uk/travel Both Bus and Rail information is available on the TBC Hotline 0891 910910.

INFORMATION CENTRES

Lancashire County

Accrington	01254 872595
Burnley	01282 423125
Chorley	01257 241693
Clitheroe	01200 442226
Fleetwood	01253 772704
Lancaster	01524 841656
Leyland	01772 621857
Morecambe	01524 582808
Nelson	01282 698533
Ormskirk	01695 579062
Preston	01772 556618
Rawtenstall	01706 213677

Blackburn with Darwen Borough
Transport & Local Information Office 01254 681120

Lancaster City

Lancaster	01524 32878

West Pennine Moors

Great House Barn	01204 691549
Jumbles	01204 853360
Roddlesworth	01254 704502
Clough Head	01706 830162

Wyre District

Garstang Discovery Centre	01995 602125